1999

$2.00

10-8-91

Flowers
with a *flourish*

Flowers
with a *flourish*

Floral designs for every season

Simon Lycett

LAUREL
GLEN

First published in North America in 1999 by
Laurel Glen Publishing
An imprint of the Advantage Publishers Group
5880 Oberlin Drive, Suite 400, San Diego, CA 92121
www.advantagebooksonline.com

Library of Congress Cataloging-in-Publication Data
Lycett, Simon.
Flowers with a flourish : decorating with flowers / Simon Lycett.
p. cm.
Includes index
ISBN 1–57145–641–4
1. Floral decorations. 2. Flower arrangement. I. Title
SB449.L94   1999   98–51605
745.92--dc21   CIP

A BERRY BOOK
Conceived, edited and designed by Susan Berry for Collins & Brown Ltd
Editor Amanda Lebentz
Senior designer Kevin Williams
Photography Amanda Heywood
Additional photography by Michelle Garrett

Dedication:
For Jaynie Heynes, who has always been there for me and to David, Jules, Wilbur and
Laura, for being who they are and for letting me be me. Thank you.

2 3 4 5 00 01 02 03

Printed in China

Contents

Introduction: Inspiration for Flowers 6

Inspiration for Flowers

From boxes brimming with cut flowers at the market to colorful garden blooms and wild flowers in a country meadow, the sheer beauty of shapes, colors, and textures fires the imagination.

FOR CENTURIES, men and women have looked to flowers as a natural way of expressing emotion and of providing cheer at times of sadness, a bright reminder of warm, sunny days ahead, or as a way of showing love, respect or reverence.

My life has always been a flower-filled one and I well remember the 'Albertine' roses and glorious goldenrod which grew in the garden of my parents' home, as well as the lavender hedge, the fuchsia, and tomato plants that were my grandmother's pride and joy. These early interests were to lead me into a career that has taken me along extraordinary paths–from decorating the royal box at the Royal Albert Hall in London to sewing fresh violets onto a hat for Royal Ascot, arranging flowers for weddings in the United States, and on film sets for many productions.

At a time when the pace of life seems to be quickening at every turn, I do find it most reassuring that flowers have become so popular. Many stores now stock a perfectly acceptable range of flowers, often semiarranged to save time, too. Flower stalls and florists stock a huge variety of blooms, ensuring that for the floral enthusiast these days, an arrangement need never be dull!

Fresh from the market
Buckets of fragrant 'Doris' pinks and clear blue cornflowers are put to one side in a corner of my workroom, together with bundles of highly scented lavender. Beautiful in their natural state, they will be incorporated into arrangements that make the most of their individual charms.

As the ever-changing seasons come and go, so do the varieties of flowers and foliage sent in to the flower market from around the world. In the early months of the year, following the frenetic excitement and brash colors of Christmas and at a time when there seems to be almost nothing inspiring and exciting, my heart leaps at the sight of the first small boxes packed with delicate snowdrops and violets.

Immediately inspiration comes flooding back, producing images of tightly packed posies of pristine snowdrops presented within collars of dark green ivy leaves and terra cotta pots full of fresh green moss placed in a basket covered with sweetly scented violets. Before long, the boxes of pretty narcissus are followed by tulips, all neat and bursting with color.

Harbingers of spring
Bursting with color, these bright and beautiful tulips (above) look wonderful when arranged together in a simple vase in an informal and uncontrived fashion.

Fresh and summery
Delicate, blooming pink roses (right), dainty lilies, touches of deep blue lavender, and sprigs of variegated foliage make a stunning combination, especially when seen at close quarters.

Heady and heavy crates of bright, jewel-like hyacinths arrive, providing a reminder that spring is here and that summer, with its blowsy peonies, delicate sweet peas, statuesque delphiniums and romantic garden roses, is not so far behind.

Before we know where we are, the cases of lavender are arriving, to be followed by chunky bundles of hydrangeas in every shade imaginable. Soon we spy the first bunches of rose hips, and as the mornings become colder and darker, so the autumn flowers and foliage take their turn.

With the knowledge that Christmas begins in November, all too suddenly we realize that another floral year has whizzed by, and we are eager and ready to be inspired anew by the promised goodies that are just around the corner.

Winter warmer
Deep red carnations (above) and evergreen foliage, such as holly and senecio provide a striking winter table center, decorated with slices of preserved orange.

Autumn glow
Striking red sunflowers (right), orange-red freesias, and miniature cabbages are combined in an eye-catching display that conjures up a blaze of autumnal color.

Settings
for Flowers

THE WAY in which flowers are
used within a setting makes an
immense difference. A flowerpot of
Queen Anne's lace looks as
charming and delightful as any
number of costly roses or lilies, but
each has its place, and while I am all
for people enjoying their blooms in
any way they choose, flowers will
have much more impact if they
have been selected and arranged to
complement their surroundings.

Feature Displays

Stunning decorations on a grand scale have immediate impact,
even in the smallest of homes — they also allow you to be much
bolder and more flamboyant with your arranging skills.

WHEN CREATING feature decorations, always consider the setting–a tall display directly in front of a window for example, may not be a good idea if it blocks out all the light. A rounded arrangement is far more suitable for a window embrasure or as a feature on a table, while a tall display will have impact in a hallway or corner, set upon a high table or pedestal. Use "grand" containers that balance the size and shape of the display.

Rounded display
The table center (left) is rounded, so balance is easily achievable. Stems of foxgloves and delphiniums, which have an upright growing habit, are arranged along the same plane. Peonies, nerines, spray roses, and snapdragons fill out the display and provide weight at the base.

Tall display
White peonies (right), regal lilies, stocks, scabious, philadelphus, single-stemmed roses, sunflowers, and spray roses are among the blooms used to create this impressive display. The base consists of six blocks of flower foam, secured inside a bucket with chicken-wire. The "stone" urn is made from lightweight, easily movable fiberglass.

Small Tables

Narrow tables against walls are ideal for decorations when space is at a premium. Avoid protruding displays that can easily be knocked, and be adventurous with flat, tall, or wide arrangements.

T HE FLOWERS used in these decorations are very short to create sculptural and rather clipped effects. Overly fussy, full arrangements would look out of place on a small table, which will be lost beneath a flurry of flowers and foliage. Bold, striking displays on a simpler and smaller scale will make a greater impression. The decor of the room can also play a part in your choice of display: Here, the more romantic setting on the right required a decoration with an element of softness. The sculpture of fresh rose heads (below) is ideal in a minimalist, contemporary setting, which suits a more dramatic treatment.

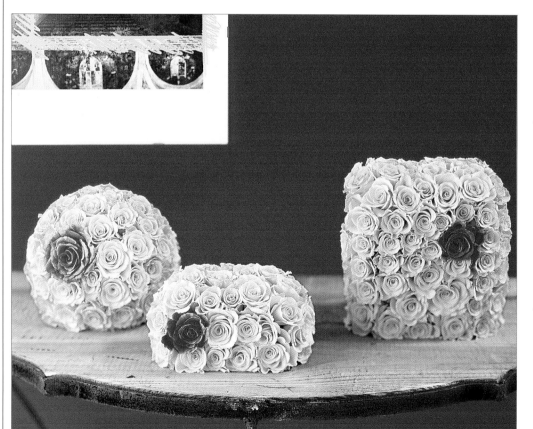

Modern rose balls
Lush and luxurious, the bases of these decorations (left) are a sphere, a block, and a halved block of soaked flower foam. Roses are cut short and inserted into the foam. A single orange flower in each block adds focus and a link to the color of the decor.

Hyacinth basket
A plain basket (right) has been bound with fresh moss into which white hyacinth flowers have been attached with wires. The basket takes time to create, but is worth the effort on special occasions, such as Easter, when it looks wonderful filled with foil-wrapped chocolate eggs.

Table Settings

*From dainty pots of garden flowers to bowls filled with the best
that the florist has to offer, arrangements on the table will set
the tone for a special event.*

RESTRAINT IS A key word when designing table arrangements, as there is nothing more irritating than having
to search for the cutlery and cruet amid a sea of flowers and
foliage. On small tables, the displays should be kept fairly low
in order to allow a clear view of fellow diners. Taller, more
flamboyant decorations are suitable for large tables where
diners do not converse across the table.

Summer strawberries
*Fresh and informal (left),
strawberry leaves and lady's-
mantle (Alchemilla) are
arranged with mixed pink
roses in strawberry patterned
tea glasses. This display is
ideal for long, narrow tables as
the glasses can be dotted
around the center of the table
amid glasses and condiments.*

Formal richness
*For a formal dinner (right),
this elegant decoration of calla
lilies, California poppies,
delphiniums, roses, peonies,
lilac, euphorbia, and rosemary
relies on dramatic color to
create impact. By mixing a
varied range of flower shapes
and textures in rich and
vibrant tones, the sumptuous
surroundings are enhanced.*

Windowsills

Potted plants are often far more suited to a bright windowsill than cut flowers, especially if they are sun-lovers, as they will thrive in the natural light.

WINDOWSILLS ARE natural perches for potted plants and a good place for simple, unobtrusive decorations that reflect the natural greenery outside. One point to bear in mind is that if the window is opened, the breeze will cause the plants to transpire more quickly and they will therefore require more frequent watering. Fragrant flowers and plants are ideal choices as their perfume will gently permeate a room, adding a caring touch. If you have an unsightly view from the window, why not plant a climber, such as stephanotis, in an internal window box and train it up a bamboo cane or trellis support. This will rapidly create a green, scented screen that will be far easier on the eye than dull lace curtains!

Berried treasures
A plain glass cake stand (left) is used as a display stand for tiny terra cotta pots filled with novel mind-your-own-business plants, each bearing minute, bead-like orange berries that match the coloring of the pots.

Spring plate
A delicate spring garden of bulbs (right) is created on a dinner plate. Fresh green moss is used as a source of moisture to sustain the flowering bulbs and plants used. The addition of small clusters of gravel or terra cotta shards adds to the effect.

Fireplaces

Flowers may be used to great effect to enhance and cheer up empty, gaping voids in a room, such as an unused fireplace. Both fresh and dried materials make delightful decorations.

WHEN ARRANGING flowers for the fireplace, it is vital to remember that the finished decoration will be seen from above, as most hearths tend to be at or near floor level. Such a decoration should be created *in situ* so that you can periodically stand up and take a few steps back to view it from strategic angles. This will allow you to ascertain which areas are more on show, thereby avoiding using all your most cherished and expensive blooms low down at the front where they will only really be seen by someone who is prostrate on the carpet!

Dried assortment
An unused fireplace (left) is the ideal receptacle for a semi-permanent decoration of dried flowers. The display is created within the grate using a ball of chickenwire attached with reel wire as if it were a normal container.

Fresh delphiniums
During the summer, this rustic fireplace (right) has a simple decoration filling its void. Tall stems of mixed garden delphiniums are casually arranged in a contemporary glass vase. An old tin bucket or stone jar would give a more traditional but equally informal effect.

Flower Arranging Basics

STARTING WITH the essential equipment needed to create floral decorations and the types of containers to use to achieve different styles and looks, this chapter gives you all the basic information you will need to create successful flower displays. There are ideas for making the most of a single bunch of simple flowers, using foliage to its best effect, teaming foliage with flowers, and creating stunning color-schemed and front-facing displays.

Containers

From a chic, modern glass vase to a simple rustic basket, the container you use makes an immense difference to the look of an arrangement, stamping it with a certain style or sense of occasion.

ALTHOUGH YOU will need a selection of vases and containers at hand when creating floral decorations, you do not have to spend a fortune on them. Empty, washed tin cans, for example, can be covered with fabrics, natural materials, such as pressed leaves, or given interesting paint effects. A glass vase is given a new look simply by adding a few drops of food coloring into the water, or a handful of colored marbles, fresh kumquats, or even scrunched-up cellophane.

Table settings
A deep wire basket is useful for larger-scale table centers, while single pots or pretty bowls filled with individual flowers or specimen plants suit smaller ones.

Informal
Wooden planters, wicker baskets, terra cotta pots, and galvanized buckets all have an earthy and rustic feel, which is perfect for casual arrangements.

Formal

A statuesque urn makes a distinctly formal statement, as do elegant china vases or bowls, with silver beakers adding a formal note to even the most humble of garden flower posies.

Modern

Frosted glass, metal, aluminum, and clear glass are spartan, minimalist, and up-to-date. Look out for clean-cut and unfussy shapes—square and cubed vases are particularly stark and contemporary.

Simple and inexpensive

Many household items can double as vases. Here a waxed paper cup has been covered with thick cotton cord, for example. A piece of cut bamboo, a plastic bowl, and jam jar also make ideal containers, either left plain or wrapped in moss, leaves, or fabric.

Basic Equipment

There are a few basic tools and essentials that every floral decorator needs to have on hand—you may find some items around the house, while others are worth the small investment.

PLASTIC PLANT POT saucers, bowls, and trays are easily stored and will not deteriorate. Baskets are also durable if stored somewhere dry. However, most wire, including stub wires and chickenwire should be purchased in small quantities to ensure they are used fairly swiftly and so do not become damp and rusty. Wires are best stored in tall glass jars or watertight tins, with each gauge of wire being kept in a separate container.

The main essentials
Shown below and opposite are the tools of the floral decorator's trade. Bear in mind that materials such as water-resistant tape and sticky flower fix should be kept out of direct sunlight, or they will melt, while wet flower foam must be soaked in a bucket of water prior to use.

Staple gun

Water-resistant tape

Reel wire

Ribbon scissors

Stem tape

Sticky flower fix

Pins

Stem strippers

Basket

Plastic flower foam trays

Plastic-coated binding wire

String

Twine

Plastic saucers

2 in (5 cm) mesh
chicken-wire

Galvanized wire

Stub wires

Plastic
extension cone

10 in (25 cm) long
20-gauge stub wires

18 in (45 cm) long,
18-gauge stub wires

Dried flower
foam spheres

Wet flower
foam spheres

Wet flower
foam block

Tips and techniques

You will sometimes need to wire individual flower stems, wire clusters of flowers into bunches, or wire fruit in order to insert them securely into the flower foam that forms the base of your arrangement. These techniques are easily mastered—all that's required are stub wires of an appropriate length for your decoration.

Wiring several flowers
Bunching the flowerheads together, bend one end of wire into a hook and loop it over the stems. Twist the wire up and around the loop several times.

Wiring individual stems
Snip off the stem ³/₄ in (2 cm) below the flowerhead and insert a stub wire into the center of the stalk. Bind with sticky flower tape.

Wiring fruit
Push a thick-gauge stub wire through the fruit below the stem end. Bend the wire ends together to form one stalk and twist together.

Conditioning flowers

To help your arrangements last longer, there are some basic conditioning rules that should be followed.
• Always provide sufficient fresh, clean water and top off the arrangement regularly.
• Remove lower leaves from stems to prevent them from rotting and so from souring the water.
• Woody or fibrous-stemmed flowers and foliage will benefit from having a small split made in the newly cut stem end, as this helps them to take up water.
• If woody-stemmed plants, such as roses, have wilted, revive them by snipping 1 in (2.5 cm) off the base of the stem and plunging them into hot water. This gets rid of any air locks in the stems. Top off with fresh water and leave the flowers in a cool place for 1-2 hours.

Basic Flower Shapes

An interesting exercise for newcomers to flower arranging is to experiment with one bunch of flowers, using various containers and styles to create many different effects.

Ten stems of cheerful yellow tulips are used to create four very different styles of decoration in a variety of containers. Simply by adding a little foliage, you will see how much bolder and more traditional the decoration becomes, while the simplicity of a glass tank provides the ideal opportunity to create a minimalist tied bunch. Once you begin to experiment, the possibilities are endless.

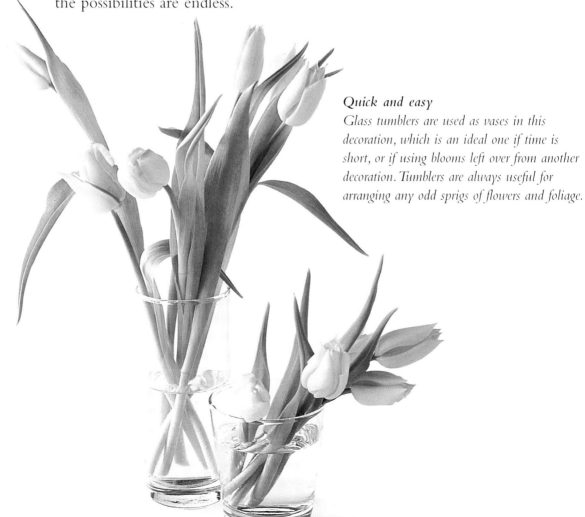

Quick and easy
Glass tumblers are used as vases in this decoration, which is an ideal one if time is short, or if using blooms left over from another decoration. Tumblers are always useful for arranging any odd sprigs of flowers and foliage.

Modern chic

The stems are bound with a rubber band, which is concealed beneath a tulip leaf and secured with a length of stem, creating a contemporary, stylish arrangement. The slim neck of the vase supports the stems.

Short and regimented

The tulips and their leaves are cut to one third of their length and placed in an upright style within a slim, oval glass vase. It is essential that the water in this vase is changed regularly as the foliage will quickly discolor it.

Roundly traditional

A spherical glass vase is always a useful container, since it looks as effective when holding only two or three flowers as it does when filled with many. Just a few stems of lady's mantle give a fuller effect and demonstrate how a little foliage can bulk out a small number of flowers.

Basic Foliage Shapes

It is easy to overlook the beautiful colors and textures that foliage has to offer, yet variegated leaves, scented herbs, and fluffy seed heads have great impact when arranged together.

THE DIFFERENT textures, colors, and forms of foliage are as varied and plentiful as cut flowers. At the foliage stage of preparing a flower arrangement, I often feel that the display looks wonderful without the addition of blooms! From squat, clipped mounds of box, hebe, and cypress to flowing, delicate grasses, fluffy lady's-mantle, and green wheat, there is a wealth of materials that can make a refreshing change from flowers.

Wintry tones
A few stems of fragrant rosemary have been added to this wintry decoration of eucalyptus leaves, dark green berried ivy, viburnum tinus, and winter jasmine to give scent and a different leaf form.

Verdant and lush
Lush green and variegated hosta leaves, stems of citrus-green euphorbia, and downy whitebeam leaves make an attractive and unusual alternative to more standard summer decorations.

Simple and striking
Sculptural and bold, this simple mound of hebe foliage looks as smart as any bowl of flowers and will last for well over a week if given fresh water regularly. Dark green box foliage could be used to create a similar effect.

Flowing grasses
A reminder of summer's end, this display of grasses, corn, and shiny burgundy hypericum berries would look wonderful as a table center for an informal harvest supper, especially with the addition of a few stems of crab apple.

Teaming Flowers and Foliage

By using flowers and foliage together in clever and creative ways, you can come up with all manner of pleasing and mutually flattering partnerships.

T HE HARMONIOUS teaming of different flowers and foliage can make all the difference to an arrangement. The colors of foliage are as marked and distinctive as the textures and it is important to consider these in relation to the colors and shapes of blooms so that everything works together as a whole. Whether you are using foliage to conceal and disguise the mechanics, or to bulk out a small number of flowers, your foliage materials should always complement your floral ones.

A perfect foil
Stems of dark green viburnum are used to camouflage the mechanics and provide a neutral background in this low, round decoration so that the attention is directed toward the colorful roses and exotic glory lilies.

Modern twist

This modern display features tall stems of pink curcuma in a glass vase, held within a collar of fresh, fluffy green moss. The moss helps to support the stems and adds a decorative flourish.

Soft touch

Short heads of flowers are arranged in a small cube of flower foam inserted into this square, frosted vase. Fluffy green lady's mantle is used to fill in and cover the mechanics and soften the effect.

Equal terms

An old terra cotta pot holds a low arrangement of flowers and flowering herbs arranged around a candle. The foliage is as important as the flowers and the addition of fragrant herbs adds an extra dimension.

Round Displays

These displays are meant to be seen from all sides, so should look balanced and well-proportioned. They are perfect on dining or coffee tables, where they can be appreciated from every angle.

E ACH OF THESE decorations has a smooth and rounded finished shape, with no jarring edges. The flowers and foliage are evenly distributed with some flowers recessed to lead the eye into the arrangement; the foliage helping to provide softness and bulk while covering the mechanics. Start off by using the foliage first to create the basic framework, and add the flowers afterward.

Autumn hues
Green wheat, crocosmia, hypericum, cotinus, and zinnia make up this autumnal display. The foliage gives a pleasing spiky effect that contrasts well with the round zinnia flowers.

Scents of summer
Jasmine, phlox, 'Doris' pinks, sweet Williams, larkspur, and chrysanthemums in lots of pink shades are perfectly complemented by fresh green hosta and lady's mantle in an arrangement that smells as sweet as it looks.

Bold impression
Strong and striking gerberas in a toning color palette are inserted into soaked flower foam in a shallow glass dish. Pebbles and shells are used to cover the foam and provide an additional decorative feature.

Winter drama
Deep red roses are set off by the textures and forms of a variety of attractive foliage, including leatherleaf (Chaemaedaphne), celosia, myrtle, rosemary, larch, and hellebores.

Front-Facing Displays

These decorations are designed to be placed with their backs to a wall or set within a fireplace. They are ideal for console tables or wherever a less bulky decoration is required.

THE MOST IMPORTANT point to remember when making a front-facing decoration is to work your flowers and foliage from the very back of the container, which will help the finished display to remain balanced and secure once *in situ*. If you are making a larger arrangement, it may help to place a few large stones into the back of the bowl, underneath the flower foam, wire netting, or other mechanics.

Formal whites
With its tumbling trails of jasmine and clusters of rich viburnum berries, this decoration in an old planter would look wonderful at a winter wedding. White spray roses have been conditioned in clean water to encourage the flowers to open for maximum impact.

Traditional summer color
This traditional decoration uses simple summer flowers and foliage from a well-planted garden. By adding single stems of various plant materials instead of lots of stems from just a few varieties, a much more informal effect is achieved.

Soft and subtle
This cheery display of wheat, corn, grasses, and seedheads has an autumnal feel. Bursts of bright yellow achillea and bold dahlias are teamed with fluffy smoke tree (Cotinus coggygria) seedheads, which soften the edges.

Color-Themed Displays

Color should always be a main consideration when creating an arrangement. Whether you are aiming for harmony or contrast, shades should work well together to create a cohesive decoration.

CLEVER COLOR combinations can really help to set the feel for a special occasion. When using blue, be aware that the deeper the shade of blue, the darker the finished decoration will be, and in poorly lit surroundings, the flowers may disappear unless teamed with pale green or soft yellow foliage and flowers. Although you should not feel too constrained by such factors as decor, very strongly colored walls or furnishings may need to be taken into consideration.

Fiery brights
This decoration features fiery orange shades, with terra cotta-colored foliage and bold hosta leaves. It exudes a feeling of sunny warmth and would cheer up any dark room or wintry dinner table.

Cool blues
This cool mixture of blues and purples is lightened by the yellow-striped irises. The simple bleached wood container also gives the display life, as its galvanized tin bindings enhance the blue shades of the flowers and foliage.

Sugary pastels
A classic combination, this sugar pink arrangement would say summer at any time of year. Using stems of year-round flowers such as lilies and alstroemeria, it may be created even in the depths of winter.

Crisp whites
Traditionally associated with weddings and christenings, all-white decorations are now considered chic and smart on almost any occasion. Care has been taken to select stems in various shades and concentrations of white, and to incorporate interesting textures and shapes of flowers and foliage to keep it from looking bland.

Spring

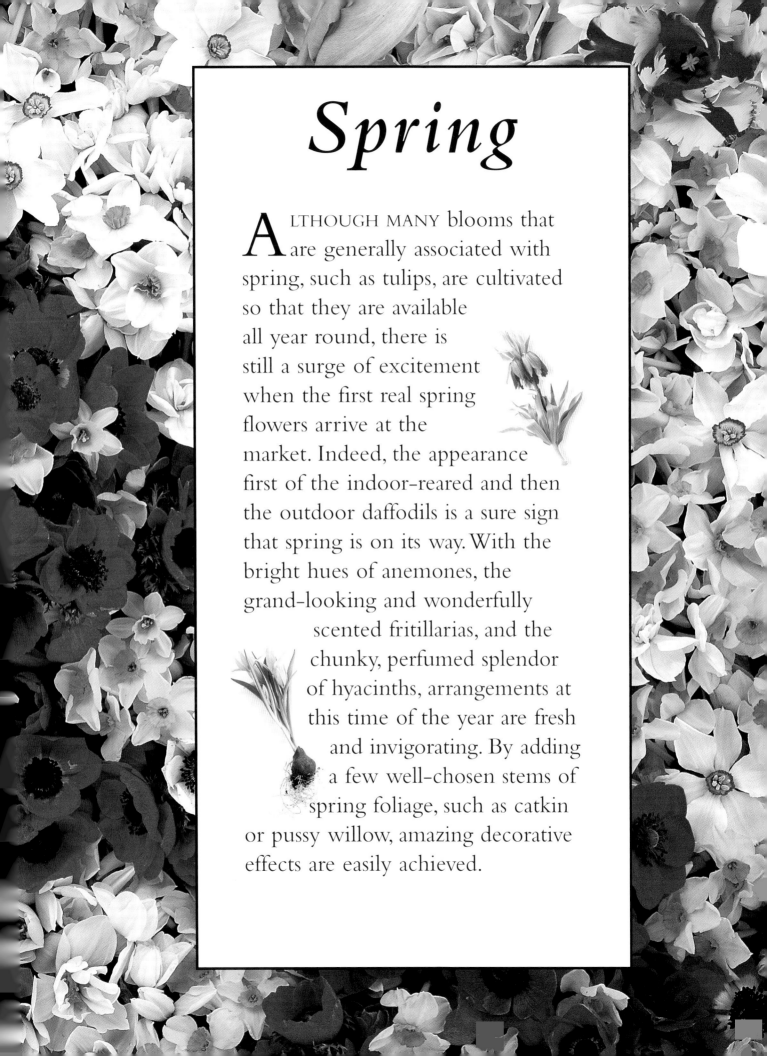

ALTHOUGH MANY blooms that are generally associated with spring, such as tulips, are cultivated so that they are available all year round, there is still a surge of excitement when the first real spring flowers arrive at the market. Indeed, the appearance first of the indoor-reared and then the outdoor daffodils is a sure sign that spring is on its way. With the bright hues of anemones, the grand-looking and wonderfully scented fritillarias, and the chunky, perfumed splendor of hyacinths, arrangements at this time of the year are fresh and invigorating. By adding a few well-chosen stems of spring foliage, such as catkin or pussy willow, amazing decorative effects are easily achieved.

Introduction

AFTER THE winter cold and the gray days of January and February, spring comes as the ultimate reward. Toward the end of March and the beginning of April, life begins to look better and more enjoyable, with the promise of longer, warmer days to come.

Once I see the snowdrops and crocuses bravely pushing their heads above the frozen and even occasionally snow-covered soil, I know that the other flowering bulbs will soon follow. With tulips and hyacinths, primroses and forget-me-nots, and myriad daffodil varieties, there are plenty of excuses for buying and arranging these lovely flowers. By mid- to late April, an entirely new crop of flowers and foliage becomes available and among these are the chunky, fat

Fragrant color
A plastic bowl containing a sphere of chickenwire is placed into a wire urn and covered with fresh green moss. Stems of mixed miniature daffodils are massed within the urn, creating a solid and fragrant block of color.

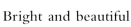

Bright and beautiful
Plump and bold ranunculus, the genteel relations of humble field buttercups, are here allowed to speak for themselves, unarranged within a couple of rough and contemporary cast aluminum vases.

ranunculus that are my particular favorites. These can be as golden yellow as butter, or as white and perfect as a bride's wedding gown. Then there are fragrant violets, lilacs, and lilies-of-the-valley, which help ensure that the arrangements at this time are among the most sweetly scented of the year. Another magical aspect of spring is that the trees, shrubs, and bushes are all coming into leaf, so for a few brief weeks, the countryside is cloaked in a million different shades of green, from the attractive citrus-green of immature birch leaves to the silver-gray colored leaves of the whitebeams. Whether you are creating a decoration on the grandest scale or simply displaying a few snowdrops on a humble saucer of moss, one thing is certain—these harbingers of spring will gladden the heart, signifying the fresh, new year ahead.

True blues
Nothing could be simpler than this decoration, comprising a couple of bunches of blue anemones placed in a blue frosted glass tumbler. On their own or mixed with different colored anemones, the effect is very striking.

Green Tulip Urn

The clean lines of a classically shaped, black basalt urn provide the perfect foil for this elegant combination of unusual green parrot tulips and frothy citrus-green viburnum.

THIS DECORATION is a classic example of the container being as important to the overall concept and design as the flowers. The same blooms, arranged within a simple country basket or pottery jug, would look much more informal, whereas in this elegant urn, the flowers take on a restrained and formal air.

Ideal as a centerpiece on a low coffee table, or even as a dining table decoration, these extraordinary green and cream parrot tulips deserve to be enjoyed and appreciated at close quarters. An interesting feature of this decoration is that its initial ordered and formal appearance will, within the space of a couple of days, become much more relaxed and spontaneous. The tulips grow and move with the light, loosening up the heart of the arrangement. This is fascinating to observe but it does mean that if a formal decoration is required, working well ahead of time would be a mistake!

Tasteful delicacy
Still formal, but slightly less so, this simple silver chafing-dish contains a delicate decoration of fresh and highly perfumed lilies-of-the-valley, supported by a slim slice of soaked flower foam and then finished with a scattering of gravel.

Making the Green Tulip Urn

So as not to damage the interior of the black basalt urn, and to enable the soaked flower foam to be securely attached, I have used a shallow plastic saucer as an inner liner for the container, taping the foam firmly in place.

The viburnum foliage is ideal for use with these extraordinary green tulips, as both have the same lime-green coloring. Viburnum also has a fairly sturdy shape, allowing you to cover the mechanics and create an unfussy background against which the tulips are seen to their best advantage. Although the foliage of flowers such as tulips, and also peonies, is often sufficient on its own to mask the mechanics used, by adding the viburnum, an additional texture and shape is introduced into the decoration. You could also experiment with different colored tulips, such as the classic flame-striped parrot tulips, or even the dramatic, deep purple 'Queen of the Night' variety.

Parrot
tulips
(Tulipa sp.)

Viburnum
(Viburnum opulus)

Materials used

Urn or similar vessel

Plastic saucer or bowl

Soaked flower foam

Sticky tape

10 stems of guelder rose

*30 stems of parrot tulips, in a
shade of your choice*

Tips and techniques

De-leafing tulips
The bulky leaves should be removed from the tulip stems in this arrangement. Although tulips' leaves can often be useful to cover the mechanics of a decoration, in this instance they will only serve to camouflage the viburnum—and it is important that these attractive fluffy pompoms are given prominence.

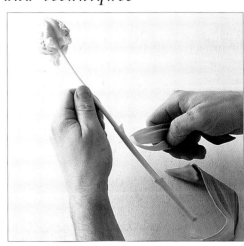

1 Tape a suitably sized piece of soaked flower foam to a saucer and place it in the urn. Add the viburnum around the edge of the container, pushing the stems well into the foam while following the outline of the bowl.

2 Add stems of viburnum to the center of the decoration, maintaining an even shape, until the foam is well covered. Use the fluffiest, most gorgeous heads within the center of the decoration, and recess some heads slightly to add depth.

3 Once the outline of viburnum is established, place the tulips throughout the whole decoration, making sure that each one is seen to its best advantage by cutting the stems a little longer so that the flower heads protrude slightly above the level of the foliage base.

4 Retain up to 10 tulips to add last. Some of these final stems should be recessed slightly to help lead the eye into the heart of the decoration, with other stems left long enough to sit slightly above the level of the others, to give the finished arrangement a soft and loose appearance.

Fresh Spring Basket

Resembling a Dutch flower painting, this basket of flowers relies upon its varied and unusual contents to make the statement, while its style of arrangement could not be more informal.

WHEN I SPOT the first bunches of majestic crown imperials (*Fritillaria imperialis*) in the market in spring, I am always deeply impressed by their regal beauty. Having not seen them for almost a year, I always forget how lovely they are, whether as cut flowers or grown in pots and borders. Those of you who know them will be familiar with their strange and pungent aroma, which is present in the flowers, leaves, stems, and even in the bulbs from which they are grown. In this decoration I have used a plethora of the most wonderful and traditional of spring flowers and foliage, arranging them all in a very casual fashion, so that the full beauty of the flowers provides the main decorative element.

Colorful collection
Camellias, apple blossom, hyacinths, snake's-head fritillaries, daffodils, and tulips create a bountiful impression in an old trug.

Making the Fresh Spring Basket

The basket for this decoration was originally too tall, so I cut off the top few inches. I then made a thick rope of fresh green moss and attached it to the neck of the basket as an extra decorative element. The flowers are an unorthodox selection, and I have used single stems and clusters of two–heresy in terms of traditional Flower Club rules, which state that nothing should ever be arranged in even numbers! The joy of this style of decoration is that there are no rules as to its content or finished look. If there are only two stems of crown imperials in the flower market, they will suffice, as will a single branch from your blossom tree. The art is in the combination of all the elements, which cannot fail to look spectacular when they are brought together *en masse*.

Hyacinth
(Hyacinthus sp.)

Camellia
(Camellia sp.)

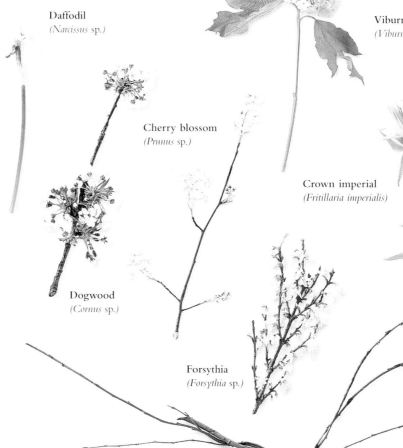

Daffodil
(Narcissus sp.)

Viburnum
(Viburnum opulus)

Cherry blossom
(Prunus sp.)

Crown imperial
(Fritillaria imperialis)

Dogwood
(Cornus sp.)

Forsythia
(Forsythia sp.)

Weeping willow
(Salix babylonica)

Materials used

Basket

Fresh green moss, 18-gauge stub wire and reel wire

Polyethylene (e.g. plastic trash bag)

Soaked flower foam

2 stems of weeping willow

2 branches of cherry blossom

3 stems of forsythia

2 stems of dogwood

3-5 stems of viburnum

3 stems of camellia

8-10 hyacinths

2-3 crown imperials

2 bunches of daffodils

1 Bind pieces of moss together with reel wire to form a garland, making sure that no ugly joins or soil patches are showing. Fix the moss band to the top rim of the basket using stub wire.

2 Line the basket with polythene and insert a block of soaked flower foam. Wind lengths of willow around the basket, using the foam to support the ends and stub wires to secure it in place.

3 Arrange the forsythia first, along with stems of dogwood, to establish the finished size of the decoration. These give height but are lightweight, so will not make the arrangement look heavy.

4 Camellias are added to give weight at the base. I have clustered them to one side of the arrangement, rather than dotting them throughout, to give them more impact.

5 Add the cherry blossom and viburnum to soften the edges of the decoration. Add the crown imperials to give a different color and leaf form. These should sit slightly above the other materials.

6 Add daffodils and hyacinths, inserting them into the foam in groups. Before inserting the thick and soft stems of hyacinth, push a piece of bamboo cane, or even your little finger, into the foam to make a hole that will take the stem.

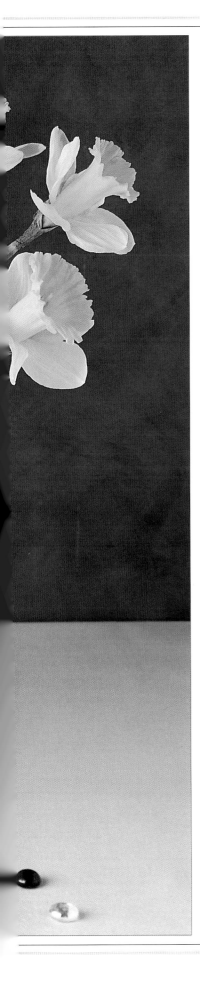

Modern

Twisted Daffodils in Marbles

The naturally straight stems of cheery narcissus are given a new twist in this futuristic decoration. Set among handfuls of blue glass marbles, these simple flowers take on an ethereal quality.

THIS ARRANGEMENT is fun to create but does require hollow-stemmed flowers, which are rare once the spring narcissus have finished their season. You could make a similar decoration with non-hollow stemmed flowers using a slightly different method. Instead of inserting the wire into the cavity within the stem, the wire can be wound carefully around and up the stems, supporting the flower head and allowing a limited amount of flexibility. I have used only one type of flower in the arrangement, preferring to let the strong forms of the narcissus and the dramatic shapes of the twisted stems make the statement in their own right. However, by combining different materials you can create many interesting shapes.

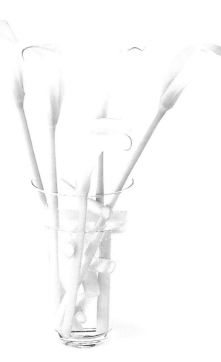

Linear lilies
This arrangement of elegant, simple, white arum lilies is very clean and modern in its styling. Lengths of spare stem are cut and wedged into the vase to support the lilies while adding a decorative touch at the same time.

Making the Twisted Daffodils in Marbles

Much of the art of this decoration is in the choice of container, which should allow the stems to be held securely but still enable them to be seen. I have used a modern etched glass and steel container, which lends itself perfectly to the style of arranging. However, a simple glass vase would also suffice, particularly one with a contemporary or unusual shape.

As with all arrangements, it is essential that the mechanics are sound and secure, especially as the balance may be rather hard to achieve with the flower stems being bent in all directions.

To secure the flower foam in the bottom of the vase, I have used a tiny, four-pronged plastic device, known as a flower foam holder or "frog." This is fastened to the bottom of the vase with a piece of waterproof, moldable flower fix. Be warned, however, that because the flower fix is extremely sticky, it can also be very difficult to remove—so I would recommend that you do not use too much! The glass marbles, which are sold for use in floral decorations, are placed on top of the flower foam to help weight it down and ensure that it is secure in the container.

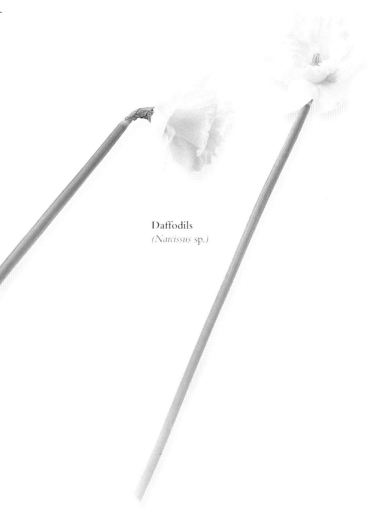

Daffodils
(Narcissus sp.)

Materials used

Glass vase or container

12-15 stems of daffodils

Glass marbles

20-gauge stub wires,
about 18 inches (45 cm) long

Soaked flower foam

Flower foam holder, or "frog"

Moldable flower fix

Tips and techniques

Wiring the daffodils
Using sharp scissors, cut off the tip of each length of stub wire at a slight angle, to create a sharp point. Insert the pointed end into the base of the stem. Then, while supporting the flower head with one hand, carefully push the wire up the stem to just below the flower head.

1 Wash and thoroughly dry the glass container before use. Attach the little plastic flower foam holder or "frog" to the base of the container using a small piece of moldable flower fix.

2 Place a piece of flower foam in water and leave until it is thoroughly soaked. Cut the wet foam to fit the container, or so that it can be wedged in securely. Add a few handfuls of marbles to completely cover the foam.

3 Having inserted a stub wire into the stem of each daffodil, insert the flowers individually into the foam. To make this easier, you can use a short piece of bamboo or a thin stick to create a "guide" hole in the foam first. As you add each stem, bend it very carefully into the desired shape.

4 Build up the design, bending the stems as you add them, and making sure that the overall shape is consistent and works within your chosen container. Sprinkle more glass marbles on top of the foam to ensure that they totally cover your mechanics.

Inexpensive

Easter Eggshells

This simple and pretty display of flower-filled eggs certainly makes a healthy change from the usual chocolate ones offered during the Easter holidays.

THIS DISPLAY is extremely easy to create, requiring neither specialist materials nor expensive hothouse blooms. You may use just about any tiny flowers or sprigs of greenery from the garden, and the result will look equally attractive.

Empty eggshells are used as containers, which cost nothing, and these are filled with a little water and little clumps of the attractive and delicate-leafed plant, baby's tears. Even those with the smallest window box of plants should be able to muster together sufficient ingredients to fill at least three or four eggs.

Materials used

Empty and cleaned eggshells

Grape hyacinths

Lungwort

Baby's tears

Johnny-jump-up

Grape hyacinth
(Muscari sp.)

Baby's tears
(Soleirolia soleirolii)

Lungwort
(Pulmonaria sp.)

Lungwort
(Pulmonaria sp.)

Johnny-jump-up
(Viola tricolor)

Making the Easter Eggshells

I have used spring flowers, but this decoration would also look charming with dainty summer blooms, such as alum root (*Heuchera*), diascia, and stems of rambling rose buds. Before use, place the flowers in water for 24 hours. The water in the eggshells should then sustain them a little longer.

1 *Crack the eggs, breaking the shell toward one end so that the other piece is as deep as possible and therefore more useful as a vase. Wash the shells and place them on paper towels to dry.*

2 *Place the cleaned and dried shells within an egg box to support them while you are arranging the flowers. Fill each shell vase two-thirds full with clean water.*

3 *Carefully break off small pieces of baby's tears without taking too much root. The pieces will survive for a few days by taking nutrients from the water through the stems.*

4 *Place clusters of baby's tears in each shell, pushing them in far enough so that they can take up water. The foliage will support the taller flower stems and hold them in place.*

5 *Arrange the flowers in a simple fashion among the foliage. You do not need to be too fussy as it is the naive charm of these decorations that makes them so special.*

Inexpensive

Anemone Cup

This easy decoration is ideal for a breakfast tray or on the tea table—so if you have an odd cup and saucer sitting in your cupboard, this is the perfect excuse to make use of them.

A MONG MY favorite flowers, and those which I always look forward to seeing when they arrive in the market, are the short bunches of anemones, or windflowers as they are commonly known. They are so delicate in appearance, yet are actually surprisingly robust flowers and their bright colors gladden even the dreariest of spring days. I have used small stems of flowering viburnum to hide the flower foam because the white flowers also serve to complement the white china. You could mix the flowers in the cup, or try different varieties, such as primulas, daffodils or even grape hyacinths.

Materials used

Cup and saucer

20 stems of mixed anemones

3 short sprigs of flowering viburnum

Soaked flower foam

Small flower foam holder or 'frog'

Moldable flower fix

Viburnum
(*Viburnum opulus*)

Windflowers
(*Anemone sp.*)

Making the Anemone Cup

I have used soaked flower foam within the cup to support the flowers and foliage but if you have an old, valuable cup, it might be wise to arrange the flowers in water, allowing the stems to support one another. For a simpler effect, you could place a small flowering plant within a shallow cup, covering the pot with fresh green moss to provide the finishing touch.

1 *Cut a piece of soaked foam to fit tightly in the cup. Secure the foam using a "frog" and moldable flower fix at the bottom of the cup and pack wedges of foam around the edges.*

2 *Cut the flowering viburnum into short stems and insert these into the foam to form a low, balanced covering which partially hides the lip of the cup.*

3 *Add the anemones, one at a time. Cut them fairly short and arrange them to create a shallow, domed profile over the top of the cup, like a brightly colored cappuccino.*

4 *Continue adding the flowers in among the foliage until the cup is full, recessing a few stems to give depth. Place the cup upon its saucer, and the decoration is complete.*

Table arrangement

Spring Garden on a Plate

This assortment of delicate, dainty flowering plants and bulbs deserves to be enjoyed at close quarters, and would look great on the breakfast table.

SINCE I FIRST visited the annual flower show in my hometown as a precocious seven-year-old and saw an entire miniature garden breathtakingly arranged on simple plate, I have been fascinated by making small gardens from miniature plants and small flowering bulbs. I generally use as many bulbs as possible, because they are able to sustain themselves for longer periods, surviving on the moisture within their swollen roots. An old-fashioned plate with a slightly deeper bowl would be ideal for this decoration, which can be enjoyed long after it has been dismantled. When the flowers have faded, you can plant the bulbs in the garden and enjoy them for years to come.

Hyacinth bowl
In a blue and white Chinese comport, flowering bulbs of Hyacinthus orientalis 'Delft Blue' are grown in bulb fiber and the arrangement completed with fresh green moss.

Making the Spring Garden on a Plate

The base for this decoration is an everyday dinner plate. The plate should as large as possible and should have a shallow bowl within its center, as this will ensure that the bulbs can be embedded more securely. Because the plants used are all in flower, this is a decoration to be made on the day it is required, especially as it is necessary to remove most of the soil surrounding the root balls. It is easiest to do this by filling a deep bucket with clean water and washing the soil and compost from the roots by swishing them around in the water.

You can use any variety of small, spring-flowering bulbs from the garden, using a hand trowel to carefully dig up small clumps of bulbs that are growing in and among other plants. (You can always replant them later.) Once the decoration is finished, spray the plants liberally with water in order to keep them looking fresh for longer.

Grape hyacinth
(*Muscari* sp.)

Crocus
(*Crocus* sp.)

Miniature tulips
(*Tulipa* sp.)

Lily-of-the-valley
(*Convallaria majalis*)

Miniature daffodils
(*Narcissus* sp.)

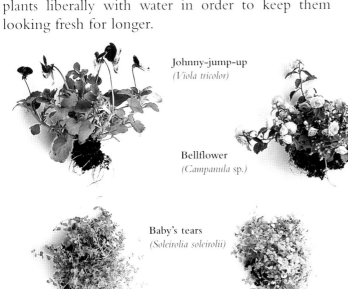

Johnny-jump-up
(*Viola tricolor*)

Bellflower
(*Campanula* sp.)

Baby's tears
(*Soleirolia soleirolii*)

Tips and techniques

Separating daffodils

Miniature daffodils are generally sold in pots of two or three bulbs. Having removed the pot, it is easy to carefully separate the indvidual bulbs by teasing their roots and gently easing them apart. The goodness stored within the bulbs will sustain them for at least a day or two.

1 Separate the bulbs and place them on a damp newspaper sheet to keep them from drying out. Position a small bellflower plant at one side of the plate to support the first of the taller bulbs.

2 Gradually build up the "garden" effect by placing the flowers and plants in small clusters, using the taller plants in the center, and the shorter ones around the edges.

3 As the shorter plants, such as the Johnny-jump-up, are added around the base of the plate, they will provide enough support to allow you to position more of the taller ones.

4 Clusters of baby's tears are used to cover the edges of the plate, at the same time disguising the root balls and bulbs, and helping to retain moisture at root level.

5 Continue to add the clusters of baby's tears among the flowers and plants until the plate is fully covered. Use a fine water sprayer to mist over the whole decoration to keep it looking fresh.

Summer

FROM HUGE, fluffy peonies
in sugar pink, creamy
white and bright cerise,
looking for all the world like
scoops of ice-cream, to
delicate scented lilies,
statuesque foxgloves, and
stately delphiniums, the
richness of summer flowers is
extraordinarily beautiful. At this
most verdant and luscious time of
year, unusual, colorful, and
inspiring blooms and lush,
resplendent greenery are in
never-ending supply.
There could be no
better encouragement
for the arranger in all of
us to take advantage of
this huge bounty and come up with
all manner of both stunning and
imaginative decorations.

Introduction

AS FAR AS I am concerned, summer has arrived when the first bunches of peonies arrive at the farmer's market, shortly to be followed by huge bunches of frothy, lady's-mantle (*Alchemilla mollis*), so called because of its delicately edged leaves. At about the same time as the peonies arrive, so too, do tall foxgloves in shades of pink and cream to mauve and even cerise. With the promise that boxes of delicate sweet peas will also soon make an appearance, every day there seems to be something new to inspire and delight.

It comes as no surprise that the summer months are the most popular time for weddings and parties. With so many flowers and plant materials available, it is possible to create some spectacular decorations: from

Pink perfection
Full-blown pink-shaded peonies are teamed with green heads of lady's-mantle in an elegant stone urn, which gives the loosely arranged materials a more formal air.

huge, grand urns that look as though they have been filled with the contents of a herbaceous border to simple terra cotta pots of strawberry leaves and crisp white daisies.

In addition to being a time of glorious and abundant color, summer is also the best time of year for intoxicating fragrances. Invisible to the eye, scent is nevertheless a valuable ingredient that gives an extra dimension to any flower arrangement. Some varieties of rose are particularly renowned for their heady perfumes, as are lilacs, sweet peas, honeysuckle and geraniums.

When incorporating several scented plants into an arrangement, the most important point to bear in mind is that the perfumes should complement one another–too many strong fragrances may clash or cancel one another out.

Refreshing blend
A traditional plethora of summer blooms, including carnations, roses, and Achillea ptarmica 'The Pearl' are arranged in a lime-green hat box, which complements the pale green summer foliage.

Contemporary chic
White delphiniums stand tall amid a base of lady's-mantle in a galvanized rectangular bucket, which has been weighed down with a few pebbles to ensure that it is stable.

Rose Topiary Ball

A delicate confection of white roses and citrus-green lady's-mantle would make the perfect accompaniment to an intimate summer dinner or a traditional wedding party.

THIS DECORATION is certainly traditional and I make no claims as to its originality. However, I feel that in our never-ending quest for the novel and the new we can often overlook tried and tested designs—and this is certainly a case in point. By using different flowers or foliage, it is possible to change the feel of the decoration: for example, white roses and many of the soft, pastel-colored flowers tend to be associated with weddings. By creating a decoration purely from roses we make a formal statement, whereas had some daisies been incorporated, a more relaxed, "country" feel would have been achieved. The same topiary, made with golden wheat, jewel-colored dahlias, and chrysanthemums would look as just striking but would be considered a far less formal decoration.

Understated elegance
Richly colored flowers and foliage are simply arranged in a treasured Victorian silver epergne. The materials are essentially very natural and informal, but by placing them in such an elegant and formal container they immediately take on a completely different air.

Making the Rose Topiary Ball

The art of creating a successful flower tree is in ensuring that the base stem and mechanics are stable, as they will need to support a considerable weight of wet flower foam and flowers. I have used a square painted tinware container that (once filled with a plastic liner) has the plaster poured directly into it, with the length of box stem set within the plaster to act as a trunk for the topiary. Whatever container you use, make sure that it is stable on a flat surface, that it is relatively heavy, and that it will be strong enough to support the weight of the plaster.

The flower foam is cut to size and then wrapped within a piece of 2 inch (5 cm) mesh chickenwire prior to being soaked. Once the flower stems are added to the foam, the wire netting will help to prevent the foam from splitting or crumbling. I have used a minimum of foliage, relying upon the roses' leaves to assist in covering the foam and concealing the mechanics. The small amount of lady's-mantle provides color contrast and has a soft texture, which lends a lighter quality to the overall design.

White roses
(Rosa sp.)

Lady's-mantle
(Alchemilla mollis)

Materials used

Stem and suitable container

Plastic liner or pot

Plaster of Paris

Soaked flower foam

Chickenwire

Stub wires

Fresh green moss

5 short stems of lady's-mantle

40 stems of short white roses

1 *Fill a plastic pot (to fit inside your container) with plaster, insert a straight branch centrally and, once the plaster has set, fix a cube of presoaked flower foam, wrapped in chickenwire, to the top of the trunk with stub wires. Cover the pot with moss.*

2 *Carefully add single stems of delicate lady's-mantle, using the larger leaves to help cover the flower foam, while the fluffy, green, lace-like flower heads will help add a delicacy to the finished decoration.*

3 *Insert the stems of roses, one at a time. Make sure that each stem is pushed securely into the foam. It is also important to work systematically around all the sides of the foam cube to keep the tree balanced and stable.*

4 *Continue to fill out the cube, aiming for an even, rounded shape. Make sure that some rose stems are cut slightly shorter and are recessed deeper into the arrangement, giving depth and adding contrast to the overall display.*

Informal

Garden Bounty

This evocative arrangement conjures up the freshness of a country garden. The flowers virtually arrange themselves, creating a relaxed shape with plenty of interesting textures.

ONE OF THE great pleasures in summer is picking flowers from the garden, and this arrangement uses many of my favorite summer blooms. The predominant color scheme is cream, with splashes of palest buttermilk yellow and pale pink. Peonies, poppies, Solomon's seal, and columbines are sharpened by clusters of lady's-mantle. This rather traditional bunch of flowers and foliage is given a contemporary twist by being arranged within a simple and modern clear glass square tank.

The joy of this style of arrangement is that it can be made using a range of different materials, either gathered from the garden, or bought from a florist. Whatever ingredients are used, the technique remains the same, and once mastered, can be used to create a variety of different looks merely by substituting different plant materials.

Dramatic color
On a larger scale, but within the same glass tank and building upon the basic framework of flowers featured opposite, more dramatically colored flowers and stems of foliage are added to create a very vibrant arrangement.

Making the Garden Bounty

Although I do provide a list of materials used for this arrangement, it is merely offered as a suggestion, for once the techniques are mastered it is possible to create many variations in a similar style using a huge range of different plants and flowers.

I particularly love to make this decoration using small stems and odd flowers and pieces of foliage gathered from the garden while I am out doing a little light deadheading or summer tidying.

The important thing to remember is that the stems need to be stripped of all their leaves, side shoots, and so on, to prevent the water from turning sour. The stems will also need to be slightly longer for this style of arranging than if they were being placed directly into flower foam.

Solomon's seal
(Polygonatum sp.)

Columbine
(Aquilegia sp.)

Peony
(Paeonia sp.)

Lady's-mantle
(Alchemilla mollis)

Roses *(Rosa sp.)*

Wheatgrass
(Agropyron)

Poppy
(Papaver rhoeas)

Materials used

Glass vase

3-4 stems of columbine

3-4 stems of spray roses

4-5 stems of Solomon's seal

5-6 stems of lady's-mantle

5-6 stems of poppies

6 stems of wheatgrass

5 stems of peonies

Tips and techniques

It is important when creating the arrangement to ensure that the flowers are in the best possible condition, and also that any surplus leaves or blemished flowers are removed before you start. A tiny drop of bleach in the water will help prevent it from turning stale.

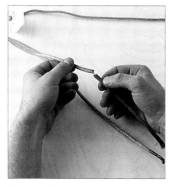

Snapping poppy stems
Snap poppy stems with your fingers, instead of cutting them, to make them last longer.

Stripping lower leaves
Remove all the leaves that will be under water, as these can encourage bacteria.

1 *Fill the vase three-quarters full with water. Using the Solomon's seal, and having stripped away the lower leaves, make a core structure in the vase to provide a frame for the arrangement.*

2 *Add some stems of lady's-mantle and then build up the framework with the smaller flowers, a stem at a time. Save the more decorative flowers until last, as they should be placed in focal positions so that they are seen to their best advantage.*

3 *Insert the stems of peonies at the base of the arrangement, where they give some weight and definition. The peonies add a boldness that would be lacking if only the softer and more delicate flowers had been used.*

4 *Clusters of spray roses are added to the arrangement, their white coloring echoing that of the peonies, but providing contrast with their delicacy. Once completed, top off the vase with water and keep an eye on its level, as the flowers drink rapidly.*

Modern

Lemon Lily Vase

Refreshing lemon-yellow and green speckled lilies are teamed with foliage and arranged in a novel fashion upon an upturned glass vase filled with fresh lemons.

THE BEAUTY OF this decoration lies in its simplicity of form: bold, perfectly shaped calla lilies and arum leaves are used to dramatic effect, while the overall style is minimalist. The upturned vase provides an extra dimension, making the decoration far more interesting and contemporary than if it had been turned the right way up in a traditional manner. I have also incorporated another modern design concept by using equal numbers of flowers and foliage. Rather than following the accepted rules of flower arranging, which require that only odd numbers of flowers should be used, here it is important to use only the number of stems that are essential to the design. In this way, the flowers themselves dictate the form.

Had additional flower heads been incorporated into the decoration, the clean and uncluttered lines would have been lost.

In the pink
This decoration would look great in a contemporary glass and steel environment. A piece of square-sectioned wire has been formed into a tube to supporting three deep pink anthuriums. The flower stems have been inserted into tiny plastic vials of water, which are concealed with a binding of green moss.

Making the Lemon Lily Vase

The choice of container is integral to the finished effect of this arrangement, and the fact that it is raised but appears to be hovering, suspended in mid-air upon the fresh lemons, makes it look all the more unusual. If you are unable to find a similar vase to the one I have used, take a look in your cupboard–any interesting and unusual stemmed glasses may be ideal when turned upside down. If they are stable when inverted and there is sufficient room for a small piece of flower foam to be attached to the base of the stem, you can improvise with all manner of containers.

The dramatic quality of the plant materials is another essential feature of this decoration. I have used bright yellow calla lilies and very sculptural speckled arums, with delicate yellow kangaroo paw and soft lady's-mantle adding lightness. In the autumn, many of the dramatically tinted leaves would be ideal for such an arrangement, perhaps combined with clusters of shiny berries and fruits.

Materials used

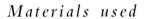

Glass vase

Soaked flower foam

Water-resistant tape

5 stems of yellow-speckled calla lilies

2 arum leaves

1 stem of kangaroo paw

2 stems of lady's-mantle (with several leaves)

2 stems of green love-lies-bleeding

Kangaroo paw
(*Anigozanthos flavidus*)

Love-lies-bleeding
(*Amaranthus sp.*)

Lady's-mantle
flower head
(*Alchemilla mollis*)

Lady's-mantle
leaf (*Alchemilla mollis*)

Arum lily
(*Zantedeschia aethiopica*)

Arum lily leaf
(*Zantedeschia aethiopica*)

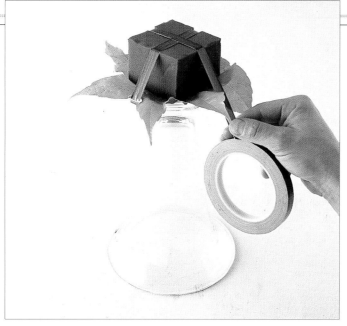

1 *Place a few lady's-mantle leaves beneath a cube of soaked flower foam upon the base of the upturned glass vase. Using waterproof flower tape, secure the foam in place, making sure that the ends of the tape are stuck securely to the glass.*

2 *Use the largest arum leaf to conceal the flower foam and form a strong, dramatic line through the design from top right to bottom left. Cut the calla lilies short and insert them centrally to provide a point of focus.*

3 *A tall stem of kangaroo paw is added to provide some height. It also serves to link the placement of the tallest arum lily at the top of the arrangement to the others within the design.*

4 *Leaves of lady's-mantle are placed within the centre of the arrangement to conceal the flower foam. Stems of green, trailing love-lies-bleeding are added at the right-hand side to finish off the decoration.*

Inexpensive

Flower Bowls

These appealing flower-filled bowls are extremely simple and yet look so chic. Enjoy their delicate charm at close quarters, perhaps on a summer lunch or dinner table.

AN ASSORTMENT of frosted glass bowls is filled with water and fresh flowers and leaves placed upon the surfaces to float. The containers contribute much of the charm of this pretty arrangement, as they have been chosen from the same blue–purple color palette. You could also use small cups, clear glass tumblers or stemmed wine glasses. These decorations can be assembled in seconds from a few leaves and flower heads grown in even the tiniest of window boxes. If you were serving a supper which required eating with the fingers, they could also double up as finger bowls.

Materials used

Frosted glass bowls	*Wallflower*
Johnny-jump-up flowers	*Lady's-mantle*
Scented-leaved geranium	*Corydalis*
Moss rose bud	*Nemesia*
Alum root flowers	*Sweet peas*
Delphinium flowers	*Verbena*
Chive flowers	*Dill foliage*
	Catmint

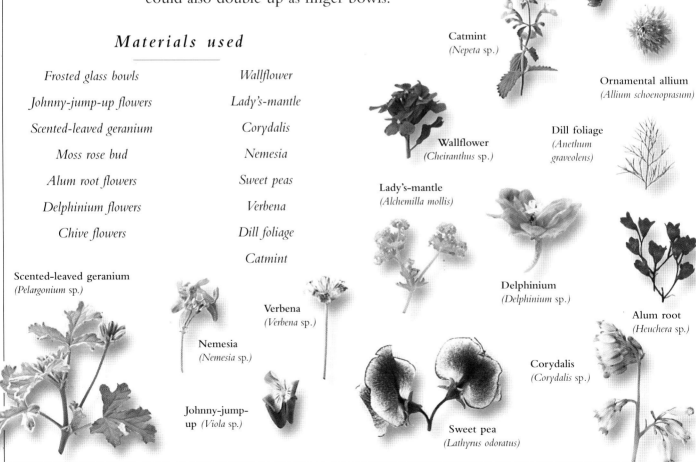

Moss rose
(*Rosa* sp.)

Catmint
(*Nepeta* sp.)

Ornamental allium
(*Allium schoenoprasum*)

Wallflower
(*Cheiranthus* sp.)

Dill foliage
(*Anethum graveolens*)

Lady's-mantle
(*Alchemilla mollis*)

Delphinium
(*Delphinium* sp.)

Alum root
(*Heuchera* sp.)

Scented-leaved geranium
(*Pelargonium* sp.)

Verbena
(*Verbena* sp.)

Nemesia
(*Nemesia* sp.)

Johnny-jump-up (*Viola* sp.)

Corydalis
(*Corydalis* sp.)

Sweet pea
(*Lathyrus odoratus*)

Making the Flower Bowls

The pleasing effect created here is due to the fact that the flowers and containers chosen are within a subtle color range of muted greens, mauves and palest pastel blues, together with touches of pink. For the best results you will need to ensure that your flowers and bowls also work together. Although I have used a selection of flowers and foliage, I have also made effective decorations using only one type of material.

1 Pour clean water into the bowls until two-thirds full. Place single heads of flowers and leaves in the bowls, either together or individually, depending on size and color.

2 Assemble the bowls in a decorative formation. A frosted glass plate makes an ideal stand, as would a piece of mirror. You could add a few tiny candles among the bowls for an extra touch.

Larkspur Candles

Fresh flowers and flickering candles are a magical combination, brought together with a minimum of expense and effort. Display one decorated candle on its own or make up a group of them.

CANDLES HAVE A wonderfully translucent quality on their own, and with stems of flowers tied around them, they look doubly attractive. Binding them with blooms is also an ideal way to disguise and cheer up any old, grubby, or marked candles.

I always have candles burning both at home and at work, and they give an extra ambiance to any setting. When used with fresh flowers there is an added dimension, for the warmth of the flame helps to release the scent of the flowers. I have used stems of pink larkspur, which have a strong upright growth and are therefore ideal for such a project. Scented flowers, such as lavender, or even foliage, such as thyme and rosemary, would also be perfect. For a more formal finish, a silk ribbon or cord could be substituted for the natural cotton cord I have used.

Materials used

1 thick pillar candle

Shallow saucer

1 bunch of pink larkspur

18 inches (45 cm) of natural cotton cord

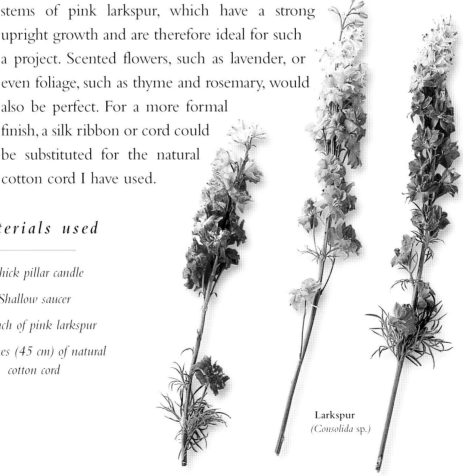

Larkspur
(*Consolida* sp.)

Making the Larkspur Candle

Although the finished candle is placed on a shallow saucer of water to allow the stems of larkspur to take up moisture, it is advisable to condition the flowers (see page 29) for a day or so before they are used. You will also need to have all your necessary materials close at hand before you start to bind the flowers onto the candle, as once you start it will be difficult to put the candle down without displacing the flowers.

1 *Sort the larkspur stems and make sure that the tips are all at roughly the same level. Holding the candle in your hand, place a few stems of larkspur against its side.*

2 *Continue adding the larkspur until the candle is evenly covered. Use the cotton cord to secure the stems, binding them firmly and finishing off with a neat reef knot.*

Table setting

Sweet Peas and Pods

This dainty decoration is something of a floral pun, with the sweet peas arranged among fresh peas in the pod. The green pods provide just the right contrast for the pastel-colored flowers.

THESE WONDERFUL, blowsy sweet peas are arranged within a simple glass bowl filled with fresh green garden peas. The arrangement would make an ideal decoration for a summer lunch, or even for the dinner table.

Sweet peas are great favorites of mine, especially now that treated cut blooms are available, as they will last for many more days than they used to. Despite this, I still love to grow a few plants myself either in pots or in a border. It is relatively easy to get good results if the plants are fed and watered properly, and once the flowers begin appearing, the more you cut them, the more will be produced. With just a little effort you can certainly grow enough plants to ensure that you have a decent supply of these most fragrant summer flowers.

Country collection
Posies of sweet William and 'Doris' pinks are arranged in small aluminum pots for a typically summery country garden display.

87

Making the Sweet Peas and Pods

Because sweet peas are such delicate blooms, they need as much care and coddling as possible, which is why I have opted to arrange them directly in water rather than in flower foam. To create this arrangement you will need two bowls, as the green pea pods will quickly rot—and cause the flowers to die—if they come into contact with water. Firstly, a piece of chicken-wire is molded into a ball shape and secured within a liner bowl with a length of reel wire. The liner bowl is then placed into the glass bowl and the fresh peas are packed around the gap in between the two, so that the inside bowl is wedged firmly in place. It is essential that there are sufficient pods to ensure that the liner bowl is thoroughly covered and thus effectively disguised.

Once the mechanics are completed, the liner bowl may be filled with clean water, ready for the stems of sweet pea flowers to be arranged within it.

Sweet peas
(*Lathyrus odoratus*)

Materials used

40 stems of sweet peas, in
mixed pastel shades

Chickenwire

Plastic bowl

Glass bowl

Reel wire

Fresh peas in pods (to cover
the mechanics)

1 *Roll a piece of 2 inch (5 cm) mesh chickenwire into a ball, place it in the plastic bowl and secure in place with reel wire. This bowl is then placed inside the glass bowl and fresh peas are used to wedge it into place.*

2 *Pour clean water into the plastic bowl until two-thirds full. Start to arrange the sweet peas, placing them into the bowl in clusters of two to three stems of one color at a time. Allow the stems to reach well into the water and to be supported by the wire.*

3 *Continue adding the sweet peas so that they begin to cover the rim of the bowl. As more stems are added they will begin to support one another. Cut one or two stems fairly short and recess them among the others to help conceal the mechanics and at the same time give a feeling of depth.*

4 *Sweet peas look best arranged with either a minimum of foliage or none at all, so continue recessing a few flowers of each color to hide the mechanics without having to introduce any leafy distractions. Continue until a regular profile is achieved and there are no obvious gaps.*

Autumn

JEWEL-LIKE BERRIES, shiny crab apples, and the warm, earthy hues of autumn leaves and flowers create a vibrant tapestry at this time of year. The dazzling shades of summer may have faded, but that does not mean resorting to hot-house blooms and imported flowers and foliage to create colorful decorations – autumn has a rich and varied harvest all its own. Fallen leaves, bare twigs, and simple garden chrysanthemums, or even dahlias spared from early frosts, are among the many ingredients that can make up a wonderful seasonal display to grace a winter dinner party table, or perhaps, become a centerpiece on a coffee table or occasional table.

Introduction

A S THE EVENINGS grow shorter, the days grow darker, and the trees become bare and stark, you may feel that this season has little to recommend it. Yet I think of autumn as a magical time, a gentle way of easing us into the cold winter months as the earth rests and we enjoy the good things we have stored away in the lull before the excitement of Christmas.

I associate harvest time with golden corn; long walks through brilliantly colored leaves; crisp, clear mornings; and all the warm colors of chrysanthemums, shocking pink nerines, and bright berries, glistening beneath an early morning hoar-frost.

Born and brought up in a small country town, I grew accustomed to a rural landscape. Even my daily walks to and from school took me through wonderful park land, where I would be surrounded by trees and hedges and often delayed as I stopped

Wreathed in rust
A garland of beech leaves and double garden chrysanthemums are wound around the stem of a rusted iron candlestick. The colors are so sympathetic that the garland could almost have been cast from the same metal.

Casual charm
Autumn leaves from a plane tree are wrapped around posies of spray chrysanthemums and secured with raffia. They are then pushed into a container of soaked flower foam within this rustic wooden crate to create a casual, natural effect.

to collect beechmasts and pine cones. It is a habit which I have failed to break, for I find it virtually impossible not to pick up fallen cones and nuts, and even autumn leaves, the colors of which are amazingly vibrant and varied. One of the greatest pleasures of this time of the year is that it is possible to create the most colorful and original of decorations from leaves and twigs collected from the garden. With or without flowers, the effects will be marvelous.

As you stroll around the garden or countryside, look down at the leaves on the ground and you will be amazed at the wealth of colors. These, when combined with suitably colored containers and a minimum of creative skill, will allow you to create interesting and attractive decorations, which have the extra magic of being made from materials, that are rare, in that they are available only for a few months of the year.

Clear and simple
This frosted glass bowl in a steel stand contains upright stems of red dogwood, with a collar of hydrangeas covering the exposed flower foam. Deep claret-colored lilies are added to echo the lacquer-like tones of the twigs.

Formal

Burgundy Rose Bowl

Deep red berries, burgundy red and orange roses, and euphorbia spill out from an elegant china bowl in a sophisticated arrangement with a rich and opulent feel.

FORMAL ARRANGEMENTS can often appear rather stiff and contrived, but it is easy to avoid this by choosing your ingredients well. Here, I have teamed cotoneaster berries and elegant sprays of euphorbia to lend a softer feel to the arrangement, which sits perfectly in a Wedgwood china bowl decorated with a deep burgundy motif. Only one type of flower is necessary to create a formal yet naturalistic effect, and I have chosen open heads of roses because they add a sophisticated flourish and are perfectly framed by the more simple country foliage.

As a concession to the season, deep orange and burgundy are the colors I have selected. Yellow and deep cream would work equally well in this decoration, as would blood red. To create additional interest, short stems of red dogwood are included to provide just a touch of texture in among the more rounded forms of the flowers.

Understated elegance
The same principles apply to this modest decoration, arranged within a Shaker style wooden box containing a plastic waterproof liner. Lilies and garden chrysanthemums are used among stems of spindle berry and hypericum, types of foliage that work particularly well with wood.

Making the Burgundy Rose Bowl

I used soaked flower foam as the base for this decoration, because I did not want to damage the inside of the china bowl. If you are using a less precious container, you could use chickenwire as the base. Whichever you choose, ensure that the base is sound and secure (florist's tape is ideal for attaching materials to ceramic and glass) prior to arranging.

The framework of foliage is created using one type of material at a time, with the bulkier hypericum leaves helping to cover the mechanics first. The dogwood is added next, just slightly proud of the decoration, giving a gentle spiky effect, placing the euphorbia around the sides to soften this look. The roses should be added last as they are the star performers. Recess a few of them to give depth and help lead the eye into the arrangement.

Burgundy rose
(*Rosa* sp.)

Dogwood
(*Cornus* sp.)

Orange rose
(*Rosa* sp.)

Euphorbia
(*Euphorbia* sp.)

Hypericum
(*Hypericum* sp.)

Materials used

China bowl

Soaked flower foam

10 stems of hypericum

3 stems of dogwood

6 stems of euphorbia

20 stems of orange roses

6 stems of burgundy red roses

Tips and techniques

Sealing euphorbia
Euphorbia has a milky sap which can be an irritant, so exercise caution when handling it. By sealing the cut end of the euphorbia, you can prevent the sap leaking and prolong the life of the stem. Light a match and hold the end of the stem in the flame for a few seconds, before plunging it into cold water.

1 *Insert trimmed stems of hypericum into the flower foam to form the framework of the design, using the leafy off-cuts to help cover the foam. As with all hard-wood plant materials, the stems should be cut and split slightly to aid them in taking up water.*

2 *Add the short stems of shiny red dogwood throughout the arrangement, but avoid making the central ones too tall. They should be allowed to protrude just slightly above the hypericum.*

3 *Use the euphorbia around the edges of the arrangement, to gently cover the sides of the bowl, with one or two stems being used in the center, again making sure they are not too high.*

4 *Add the roses among the foliage, grouping them in several places, rather than dotting them throughout the arrangement, to give them more impact. Some are cut shorter and pushed in among the foliage to provide depth.*

Informal

Country Basket

Brimming with garden foliage and flowers, this colorful basket provides a warm welcome on a crisp autumn day. Shiny pink pomegranates add an exotic touch.

WHAT BETTER WAY TO enjoy all that the autumn garden has to offer than by gathering seasonal foliage and flowers and arranging them informally in a simple rustic basket? In this case, I have used an old bicycle pannier which I found in a small junk shop many years ago. The basket's large, square base makes it very stable, which is ideal for this type of front-facing arrangement.

This decoration was designed to stand on the floor in a hallway, providing a welcome for guests, perhaps as they arrive for a simple harvest supper. However, you could adapt it to any situation in the home, using a smaller basket for a shelf or table, or even a larger one for the hearth or kitchen where there is plenty of space. The beauty of the display is that it virtually arranges itself. Long and short stems and branches of berried foliage and autumn leaves act as a frame to stems of simple garden flowers. With the addition of succulent pomegranates, the whole basket becomes a celebration of the fall season.

Ornamental pot
The earthy color of terra cotta makes it an ideal companion for plant material gathered at this time of the year. Here, ornamental cabbages (resembling giant rose flowers) are teamed with shiny ornamental peppers and garden berries. A thick cream beeswax candle adds a warm glow.

Making the Country Basket

A front-facing arrangement such as this must be created within a stable container, as the weight will always fall to the front of the design, no matter how carefully you arrange the materials. It is also important to start at the back of the container and work toward the front to keep the whole as balanced as possible. When selecting your materials, no rules need apply–in fact the wilder and more informal the branches, the better. Don't worry if you have only single stems of certain materials as this will enhance the natural feel of this decoration. If you cannot cut flowers from your own garden, ask your florist to order suitable home-grown flowers. Local growers often sell off cut flowers in autumn as they empty their greenhouses in preparation for the new season. Such blooms are ideal.

Spray chrysanthemums
(Chrysanthemum sp.)

Bloom chrysanthemum
(Chrysanthemum sp.)

Hydrangea head
(Hydrangea sp.)

Pomegranate

New York aster *(Aster novi-belgii)*

Berried ivy
(Hedera sp.)

Cotoneaster
(Cotoneaster sp.)

Materials used

*Basket or rustic container
and plastic bucket*

*Piece of chickenwire,
24x24 inches (60x60 cm)*

Stub wires

Sphagnum moss

*5-7 stems of cotoneaster,
in varying lengths*

3 stems of berried ivy

4 pomegranates

*10 stems of English spray
chrysanthemums*

2 heads of hydrangeas

*7 stems of bloom
chrysanthemums*

*3-5 stems of
New York aster*

Tips and techniques

Ensure the pomegranates are sound and firm – they are better under-ripe than over-ripe. When you buy large bloom chrysanthemums, they usually have small plastic bags covering and protecting the petals. It is essential to remove these quickly to prevent any moisture build-up which could cause decay.

Wiring fruit
Push a thick-gauge stub wire through the fruit below the stem end. Bend the wire ends together to form one stalk.

Using chrysanthemums
Remove the plastic from the chrysanthemum and gently open out the petals before arranging.

1 Cut down a plastic bucket to fit inside your basket, then form the chickenwire into a ball and place it in the bucket. Put the bucket into the basket, using sphagnum moss to wedge it in place. Attach stub wires through the chickenwire and to the edge of the basket to ensure the basket is secure.

2 Fill the bucket two-thirds full of water and add the foliage, one variety at a time. Use taller stems of cotoneaster first, to create an informal frame. Don't forget to add foliage at the back of the bucket to give it balance.

3 Add stems of ivy, to give weight to the base of the decoration and to obscure the wire and foam, then wire the pomegranates into place. Group them at the front of the basket, where they will have more impact.

4 Add the spray chrysanthemums next, ensuring that the stems are pushed well into the bucket, so that they are touching the water. The chickenwire provides support and, as more flowers are added, the stems will support one another.

5 Finally, arrange the bloom chrysanthemums within the decoration. As they are your focal flowers, try to make them stand slightly above the existing materials, although you should retain at least a couple of heads to be recessed slightly into the arrangement to give depth.

Modern

Nerine and
Crab Apple Pumpkin

A bright orange pumpkin makes an impressive and unusual vase, within which clusters of shiny crab apples and vibrant nerines form a stark and contemporary decoration

INSPIRED BY a visit to the United States, for this decoration I made use of a magical vegetable that features in Halloween and Thanksgiving decorations in just about every American home. The pumpkin I have used is enormous but you can, of course, scale down the arrangement to suit a more modest-sized vegetable. You need not be restricted by the type of vegetable you use—marrows, gourds and squashes all make marvelous natural vases.

Nerines, their tall, slender stems topped by flowers in every shade from lipstick pink to coral, are ideal blooms for this arrangement, which needs no other foliage than a few stems of arching bear grass. Stems of crab apples conceal the mechanics of the decoration, add weight at the base and echo the shape of the pumpkin. Any similar heavily berried stems would be ideal.

Flower-filled gourds
Knobby gourds can be used as vases too. Slice off the base of the gourd and cut through about one-third of the way down the vegetable. Scoop out the seeds and insert soaked flower foam into which clusters of flowers are arranged.

Making the Nerine and Crab Apple Pumpkin

It is essential that the pumpkin used is fresh and sound and large enough to hold a suitable container into which the flower foam will be secured. Other vegetables, such as marrows, bottle gourds, and squashes may be used as vessels too. I have even used rutabaga and large red-skinned potatoes in the past, although hollowing these out can be hard work and rutabaga in particular tend to become smelly rather quickly.

Any flowers could be used for this arrangement, although if they are on an unfussy and foliage-free stem, the modern and dramatic effect is much easier to achieve. Nerines come in such magical colors and the contrast of their cerise and pink shades with the orange of the pumpkin makes for a very striking effect.

If you are unable to obtain sprays of crab apples, individual fruits may be used, simply by wiring them into small clusters (see page 29) before adding them into the flower foam. Branches of heavily berried cotoneaster with the leaves removed would also look wonderful.

Sotol
(Dasylirion sp.)

Nerines *(Nerinus bowdenii)*

Crab apple
(Malus sylvestris)

Materials used

Pumpkin

Plastic container to fit inside pumpkin

Sharp knife

Spoon

Soaked flower foam

Florist's tape

8 sprays of crab apple

25-30 stems of nerine

20 stems of sotol

Tips and techniques

Cutting the pumpkin
Use your waterproof container as a template for cutting out the top of the pumpkin. As the skin is rather tough, use a sharp knife to score around the bowl first, then cut straight down around the marked line and gently ease out the cut portion.

1 *Remove the marked circle from the top of the pumpkin. If necessary, remove a slice from the base so that it is stable. Use a spoon to scoop out the seeds and flesh until the plastic liner bowl fits inside the cavity.*

2 *Fill the plastic bowl with soaked flower foam, securing it with florist's tape, and place in the hollowed-out pumpkin. Cut the sprays of crab apple into short lengths, snipping just above the fruit to prevent unsightly sticks poking out. Insert the stems around the rim to mask the foam.*

3 *Push the flower stems into the foam in between the apples. Try not to put them too prominently in the middle of the "vase," as this creates too triangular a shape. Cut some flowers shorter and place them deeper within the arrangement, just sticking out from the crab apples, to give depth to the display.*

4 *Add a few stems of sotol in among the outer stems of flowers. Sotol gives a very graceful, light and airy feel to an arrangement, and here it gently softens the edges and adds a finishing flourish.*

Leaf-Wrapped Vase

Perfect for displaying a few stems of flowers, and simple and inexpensive to produce, this charming leaf-covered vase would make a lovely gift.

THIS SIMPLE vase started out as a powdered baby milk tin, an ideal container because it is watertight and tall enough to make a sensibly sized vase. You may use any similar empty container as long as it is robust. Even non-watertight vessels may be used, if a glass tumbler or jam jar is placed inside to hold the water.

When I collected the leaves for this project, they were still relatively damp. Having wiped them with a damp cloth, I pressed them between the pages of a large book (a telephone directory is also ideal for this). I then placed some heavy weights on top and after three days the leaves were ready to be used. Try to collect a selection of different-sized and colored leaves, as this makes for a more interesting finished look.

Materials used

Empty powdered milk tin, or similar

Selected pressed leaves

Double-sided tape

Spray varnish

10 stems of orange, yellow, and red carnations

1 or 2 hydrangea heads

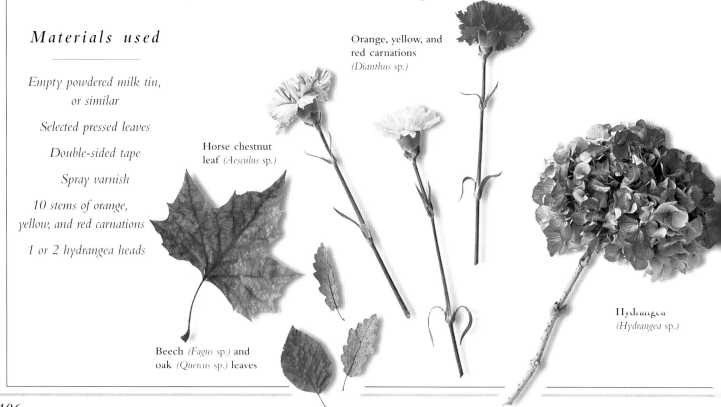

Orange, yellow, and red carnations
(Dianthus sp.*)*

Horse chestnut leaf *(Aesculus* sp.*)*

Beech *(Fagus* sp.*)* and oak *(Quercus* sp.*)* leaves

Hydrangea
(Hydrangea sp.*)*

1 *Cut up small pieces of double-sided sticky tape and attach two or three pieces to each of the larger leaves. Press the leaves into position on the side of the tin. The aim is to cover the tin—leaves overlapping the top and base can be trimmed later with scissors.*

Making the Leaf-wrapped Vase

Wash and thoroughly dry the tin prior to use. If you are worried that it may not be watertight, dry its base, place it upon a paper towel and fill it with water. After a couple of hours, check that the paper towel remains dry. Attach the leaves with double-sided tape, sticking on larger leaves first, to fully cover the tin, and then adding smaller ones among them to give variety and interest. A spray of clear varnish adds luster to the leaves. Heads of carnations are arranged in the vase, with a hydrangea or two to soften the edge.

2 *Attach a single piece of cut tape to each of the smaller leaves. Using just one small piece of tape will allow these leaves to remain almost free-standing above the larger ones. Once the tin is covered, apply a light spray of clear varnish to give a protective coating.*

Birch Pot with Twigs

Nothing could be simpler than this arrangement, which will last for many weeks. The delicate coloring of the silver birch logs contrasts subtly with the spiky willow and alder branches.

WHEN OUT WALKING, or cutting logs for the fire, look out for any unusually colored or marked bark with which to make this unusual arrangement. I have used slender poles from a silver birch sapling, but thicker branches are just as easy to work with if you split them in half lengthways.

The twigs come from an alder tree, and the catkins on them give an added effect. Of course, you do not have to reproduce exactly the look I have created here, you could also use this container for flowers and/or various types of foliage, either with or without the twigs.

Materials used

Plastic pot, with relatively straight sides

Sticky flower fix

Flower foam

12 sawn lengths of tree branches, each about 9 inches (23 cm) long

Reel wire

Raffia

10 alder twigs

10 willow twigs

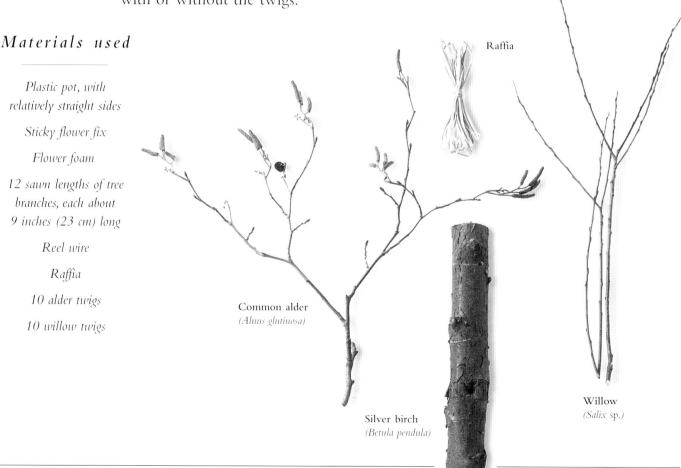

Raffia

Common alder
(Alnus glutinosa)

Silver birch
(Betula pendula)

Willow
(Salix sp.)

Making the Birch Pot with Twigs

Many trees and shrubs develop beautifully colored barks at this time of year, which can be used to great effect in this arrangement. Look for branches that are fairly smooth and straight, so that they can be attached easily to the container, and will not stick out at ugly angles. Once secured in place with the sticky flower fix, reel wire is tied around the poles for added security.

1 *Saw the poles into lengths 1 inch (3 cm) taller than the container that is to be covered. Don't worry if the poles differ in length slightly, as this adds charm to the arrangement.*

2 *Measure a length of sticky florist's fix, attach it to the top lip of the pot, and remove the protective paper covering.*

3 *Press each pole against the side of the pot and into the flower fix. Once the pot is covered, wrap around several lengths of reel wire just below the middle of the poles and tie.*

4 *Finish off with a generous swag of raffia, tying it around the pot so that it covers the reel wire. Arrange the twigs and branches loosely within the pot.*

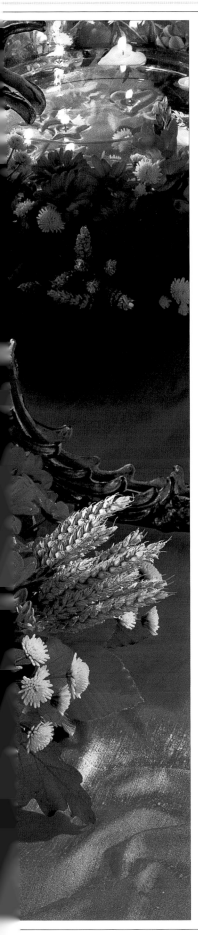

Table setting

Harvest Flower Ring

Tiny floating candles shimmer in a water-filled glass bowl and cast a flickering light on the surrounding ring of autumnal flowers, foliage, ears of golden corn, and berries.

CANDLELIGHT ALWAYS adds atmosphere and warmth to a dinner table, its soft, flattering light turning any meal into a special occasion. Flowers and a variety of foliage also help to make the table special, and by combining the two in an original way, spectacular results may be achieved.

The flowers and foliage used for this decoration are all simple garden varieties, and yet they look incredibly exotic and rich when arranged in this fashion. I have chosen to mix the varieties and colors of flowers within my table setting, but by using one type or color, you can achieve a different but equally striking look.

Berry and apple ring
Berries, crab apples, and leaves are used in a similar way to create a ring surrounding a terra cotta pot. A candle in the middle sits amid a bed of moss and apples.

Making the Harvest Flower Ring

The base for this decoration is a commercially available flower foam wreath frame. Most good florists will sell these in a variety of sizes. They need to be very thoroughly soaked before use, and warm water seems to be more easily and quickly absorbed. It is a good idea to select the bowl you plan to use within the ring prior to buying the frame, to ensure it will all fit together once finished. As the foliage and flowers used are cut quite short, you can incorporate little clippings and prunings from the garden. Even fallen autumn colored leaves may be used, mounted on a wire in the same way as the wheat.

Small sprays of yellow button chrysanthemums work well here, as they echo the centers of the daisy sprays. The golden corn also blends in beautifully with both the colors of flowers and the foliage, and it is especially evocative of harvest time.

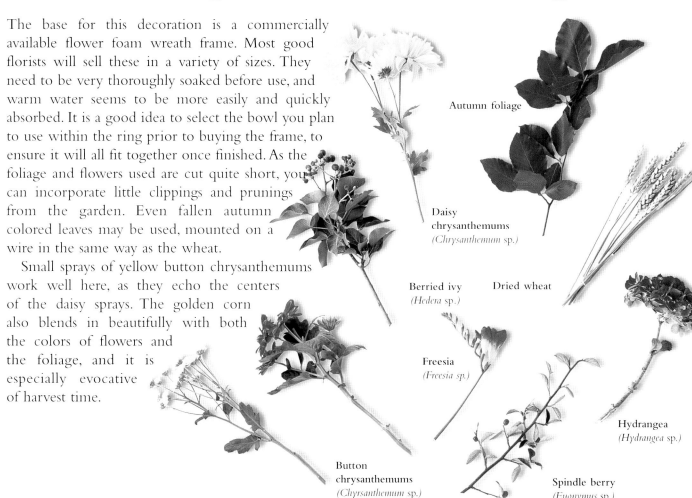

Autumn foliage

Daisy
chrysanthemums
(*Chrysanthemum* sp.)

Berried ivy
(*Hedera* sp.)

Dried wheat

Freesia
(*Freesia* sp.)

Hydrangea
(*Hydrangea* sp.)

Button
chrysanthemums
(*Chrysanthemum* sp.)

Spindle berry
(*Euonymus* sp.)

Materials used

1 flower foam wreath frame

Glass bowl

5 stems of assorted
autumn foliage

6 sprays of assorted daisy
chrysanthemums

3 sprays of contrasting
button chrysanthemums

3 hydrangea heads

4 stems of berried ivy

3 stems of spindle berry

5 stems of freesias

1 bunch dried wheat

Stub wires

Floating candles

Tips and techniques

Keeping corn dry
Dried material, such as the golden corn, should not come into contact with the wet flower foam, otherwise it will absorb water and may rot. Attach the corn, or leaves if you are using them, to stub wires and insert these into the foam so that the dried material sits above it.

1 Cover the soaked wreath frame with short pieces of foliage. These need to be inserted into the foam on all sides, to ensure that the lip of the plastic tray is not visible.

2 Add the flowers, which need to be cut relatively short and can be arranged either in clusters of one color or evenly distributed throughout the decoration. As you work, ensure that the shape of the frame is maintained.

3 Finish with the dried wheat, wired into bunches of 5-6 stems, and insert them into the foam among the flowers. Vary the angles of the bunches, so that they look natural rather than regular.

4 Place a glass bowl in the middle of the ring and fill it with clean water. Finally, add small floating candles in shades that complement the arrangement.

Winter

From beautiful dark green and deepest blue pine branches to delicate and perfectly snowy white Christmas roses *(Helleborus niger)*, winter offers the imaginative floral decorator a wealth of treasures with which to create startling decorations. It is a time to make the most of shiny nuts and berries, prickly holly, pine cones in all shapes and sizes, bare twigs and fragrant spices, such as cloves and cinnamon sticks. It's also the season for a wide range of hothouse-grown favorites such as regal amaryllis, delicate jasmine and fragrant 'Paper White' narcissus. Indeed, with such a profusion of color and greenery, winter is anything but an empty and barren time of year.

Introduction

WINTER IS A SEASON associated with many images: frosty mornings; invigorating walks; icy puddles; dark, towering evergreens; and bare branches glinting in the weak sunshine. Regarded by many as a cold and rather dismal time of year, winter really does have its compensations. For who could fail to appreciate the magical effect of a crisp frost upon a cluster of bright, shiny rosehips? It is also a time to use and enjoy many different plant materials that we tend to neglect during the rest of the year when there are so many more glamorous-looking blooms to choose from. As a compulsive collector and part-time squirrel, I look forward to the winter and the opportunity to make use of all the cones, pods, and various nuts I have accumulated. Then comes Christmas, providing the perfect

Carnation stocking
This floral Christmas stocking is made by inserting heads of rich burgundy "clove" carnations into a moss base. It would look great suspended from a mantelpiece.

Foliage ring
Red and silver birch twigs are twisted into a wreath that is threaded with fresh ivy, some berried holly, and pine. A tropical leaf forms a cone to hide a water-filled tube of flowers.

excuse for decorating and over-indulging. Many people tend to associate winter flowers with the color red, and this is quite understandable, as there are many vivid shades of red in terms of flower and berry color, and these certainly help to lift the spirits on cold, gray days. However, it is important not to miss out on the many other colored flowers and foliage, some of which is only available at this time of year. The hellebore family, for example, gives us beautiful and unusual flowers that are magical to work with—yet bloom only for a very limited period.

There is also fun to be had when incorporating other traditional ingredients so characteristic of the Christmas season into decorations, such as sticks of dark sienna-colored cinnamon; smooth, shiny chestnuts; polished pecans; and oranges studded with tiny cloves and yards of crisp satin ribbons.

Festive show
The simplest of flowers are given an original festive treatment with little in the way of extra materials. A tall tumbler or even an empty jam jar could be used instead of this glass vase.

Mini-Christmas Tree

Branches of blue pine make up this miniature tree, which is studded with perfect, deep red roses, fake rubies and other "jewels" to produce a light-hearted, yet glamorous and formal decoration.

WHEN PICTURING THE perfect Christmas tree we all tend to think of one that looks symmetrical and triangular in shape—just like the drawings we all did as children! Sadly, such tree perfection is very hard to find, especially on a small scale, as here. However, by making your very own Christmas tree and decorating it with fresh flowers, you can have perfection after all! Standing approximately 3 feet (1 m) tall, this tree would be an ideal decoration for a round table in the center of a room, or within a large bay window. It would also be practical for a buffet table, as it is tall but not particularly wide, so would not take up too much table room. If making this tree for a party, you could actually put together the basic framework a week or so in advance. Simply store the pine structure somewhere cool and then add your fresh flowers at the last minute, just prior to the event.

Classic favorite
A traditional arrangement of the winter classics, holly and Viburnum tinus, *is accented by open heads of perfect white amaryllis and some open white roses. Placed with care within a simple glass vase, this decoration evokes the feeling of a crisp wintry frost.*

Making the Mini-Christmas Tree

Creating your own custom-built tree is an easy exercise but one that requires patience, as the pine branches need to be added carefully to maintain the shape of tree. The base for this decoration is a commercially available cone of dried flower foam. These come in a variety of sizes, but if you cannot find a suitable cone, it is relatively easy to make your own by carving and shaping one from a larger block. (A word of warning if you do cut your own cone from a block of foam–it forms a fine dust that is very unpleasant if inhaled.) When buying your base, bear in mind that once covered with pine, the finished size will be increased by at least 6 inches (15 cm).

Having covered the cone in pine, you may decorate it as you please, using fresh flowers or cones, nuts, baubles, etc. You could also use foliage other than pine, but it should be able to last for a while without water. Box would be a good alternative, resembling clipped topiary once finished. I have created some very attractive trees using shiny laurel leaves, applied against the sides of the cone and made to overlap like fish scales.

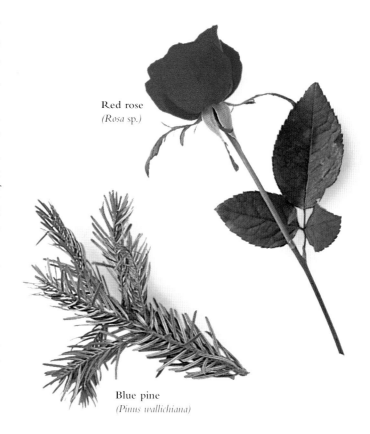

Red rose
(*Rosa* sp.)

Blue pine
(*Pinus wallichiana*)

Materials used

Dried flower foam cone

3–4 branches of blue pine

15 stems of open red roses

15 small orchid tubes

Selection of fake gemstones

Gold rose wire, or glue gun

Tips and techniques

Using orchid tubes
Extremely handy to have around, these small vials are called orchid tubes because they are used to transport orchids and tropical flowers and keep them alive on long flights to foreign markets. Each tube is filled with water and the stem of the flower is inserted through a hole in a rubber stopper at the top. The rubber then closes around the stem, sealing the water in the tube.

1 *Begin by removing the top tip of the cone. This part is often rather fragile and will weaken and almost certainly break off if filled with the rather thick stems of pine.*

2 *Remove the lower needles from the pine stems. This makes it easier to push them securely into the cone of flower foam without splitting it. Insert the first stem into the top of the cone.*

3 *Work down from the top to the center of the cone, and then up from the base, inserting the stems in levels so that they meet in the middle. In this way, you re-create the shape of a real tree.*

4 *Attach fake gems to the tips of the pine branches with fine gold rose wire, or using a glue gun. Carefully insert cut red rose stems into the water-filled orchid tubes and ensure that the rubber caps are secure. Each tube can then be pushed into the dried flower foam as if it were a natural stem.*

5 *Insert the tubes just a little way into the foam so that they are secure, allowing the pine to conceal any remaining plastic. If you push the tubes too far, you risk splitting and cracking the foam. Continue adding roses to the tree until you are happy with the decorative result.*

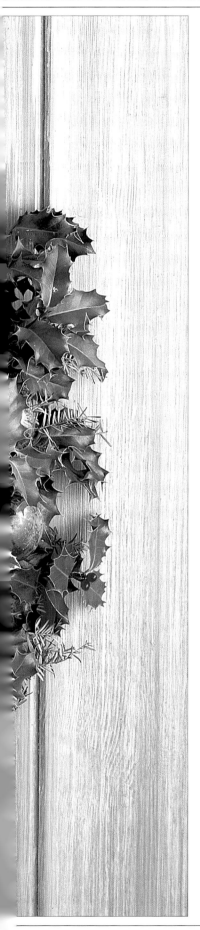

Festive Wreath

Pine cones, bright red holly berries, and shiny baubles adorn this festive wreath of greenery, finished with a flamboyant bow. Informal and welcoming, it would look at home on any door.

OW WONDERFUL IT IS, when arriving at a friend's home, to be greeted by a beautiful ring of fresh seasonal foliage, berries, and cones hanging on the front door. For hundreds, if not thousands of years, evergreens have been used as a decorative way of cheering the winter days, serving as a reminder that spring, a new year and new season are just around the corner, and with them the chance to grow fresh crops and reap in a successful harvest.

This decorative ring of evergreen foliage is merely an embellished and refined version of the much simpler bunch of foliage that would have traditionally been hung from many people's doors. It was not until the Victorian era, when there was a preoccupation with all things Roman and classical, that wreaths of foliage and flowers came to be associated with the Christmas tradition—and so the trend has continued.

Basket of lilies
Berried twigs, larch branches encrusted with small cones, trails of dark green ivy, and simple white Easter lilies (Lilium longiflorum) *form a naturalistic decoration in a basket covered with pine cones. This is an ideal winter arrangement as the lilies will last for many days and the other plants will survive for several weeks.*

Making the Festive Wreath

Timing-wise, it is advisable to start work on this project shortly after buying and putting up the Christmas tree–because any surplus branches that have been trimmed off will make an ideal base foliage for the festive ring.

Sprigs of holly, both dark green and variegated, are also important ingredients. These are extremely hard on the hands but once incorporated into the decoration, they give it a wonderfully informal and rustic feel and the number of compliments you receive will soon make you forget the pain of using them!

The base for this decoration is a wire wreath frame, which is available in a range of sizes from most good florists. If you have difficulty obtaining one, it is possible to improvise by bending a wire coat hanger into a rough circle and binding the moss around it in a similar way.

Pine *(Pinus sp.)*

Holly
(Ilex sp.)

Variegated holly
(Ilex sp.)

Pine cone

Materials used

Wire wreath frame

Damp sphagnum moss

Reel wire

Florist's stub wire

5 branches of pine

6–8 stems of holly, variegated and dark green, with berries if possible

Wide satin ribbon

20 pine cones

Wiring the pine cones

There are many varieties of pine cone, easily collected on a country walk, or purchased from good dried flower and florist's shops. Pine cones are extremely easy to use, as Mother Nature has designed them to be mounted on a stub wire with hardly any effort at all! They also last well–when they are not being used, keep them in a box somewhere dry until next required.

Mounting the cone
Holding a florist's stub wire at both ends, push the center into the base of the pine cone.

Securing the wire
Twist the two ends of wire together to create a double-pronged "mount."

124

1 *Tease the moss to remove any lumps of root or soil. Attach one end of the reel wire to the wreath frame and bind a handful of moss onto the frame. Place the next piece of moss against the first, bind, and continue until the frame is covered.*

2 *Cut the pine branches into smaller pieces and lay one or two upon the moss. Using the reel wire, bind them into position, as with the moss. Add another cluster of pine, bind, and continue around the frame, covering all the edges.*

3 *Wire the sprigs of holly in the same way as the pine cones (see left) and add them to the ring in a random manner. Push each holly cluster so that the wire appears through the moss at the back of the ring, pull it firmly into place and then bend the end of the wire and push it back into the moss.*

4 *Finally, the wired pine cones are added among the foliage, their texture and shape providing interest throughout the design. As a finishing touch, a bow of satin ribbon is added to the top of the ring.*

Modern

Rose Snowballs

Crisp, clean and contemporary, these perfect spheres are created from fresh white roses and look like huge, soft snowballs, just waiting to be thrown.

THE SIMPLEST arrangement can often be the most striking, and this is certainly true of these spheres of white roses, which could not be easier to make and yet have a very sculptural and contemporary feel. They would make a very effective table decoration, especially when placed within a very shallow urn or wine bowl. These spheres can also be made with colored flowers, although in my opinion, these should not be mixed within a single sphere as this can detract from the sculptural quality that is their unique selling point. I have made three snowballs in different sizes. Forming the base of each is a piece of flower foam carved into a spherical shape and then soaked in water. Roses are relatively bulky flowers, so they will add at least 2 inches (5 cm) to the overall finished diameter.

Sculptural drama
Berry-encrusted holly stems are wired together to form a wigwam shape. Wire coils and white orchids (Phalaeonopsis sp.) are then inserted into test tubes of water and attached to the twiggy frame with wire.

Making the Rose Snowballs

You should be able to buy spheres of foam from your local florist. If you cannot find the sizes you require, you can improvise by carving up a block of foam instead. Before soaking the foam, cut it into a cube and carve off the corners with a sharp knife. Continue shaving off the edges until it is roughly spherical. Do not worry if it is not the perfect sphere, as you will be able to rectify this once you add the flowers.

You will require a large number of flowers to cover each sphere, so you may wish to use less expensive varieties than the roses used here. Carnations or double spray chrysanthemums would work just as well. Carnations have the added bonus of lasting much longer than the roses. Whichever flowers you choose, make sure that you place them in fresh, clean water for a few hours to allow them a good drink prior to being used. This will also enable the flower heads to develop and open more fully, increasing their size so that they will cover the spheres better.

Bear in mind that water will leak from the spheres as you insert the flowers, so you may want to lay a sheet of plastic over your work surface to protect it.

White rose
(Rosa sp.)

Materials used

3 spheres of dried flower foam

Approximately 80 heads of white roses (or alternative flowers such as carnations)

Cellophane

Tips and techniques

Soaking the spheres
Oversoaking a flower foam sphere may weaken it, causing it to collapse if it is too heavy. For this reason I prefer to place the sphere in a bowl half-filled with warm water and allow the sphere to absorb the liquid, topping it off as required. When the sphere does not take up any more water, it is wet enough for use.

1 *Place the soaked sphere onto your work surface. Cut the first rose stem to approximately $1^{1}/_{2}$ inches (4 cm) in length, and insert it into the foam in the central point of the sphere. This will be the point of reference for the other flowers.*

2 *Add roses each side of the first rose, forming a line that divides the sphere in half. Handle them with care, as white petals crush easily and you could end up with a crumpled, brown ball. Work downward, leaving the base free of flowers.*

3 *Divide the sphere into quarters with a further row of flower heads. These are then infilled with roses, placed close enough to cover the foam but not so close as to overcrowd them. Make sure you retain the spherical shape as you work.*

4 *Cut out a small circle of cellophane upon which to sit the sphere. This prevents moisture seeping out and damaging the surface. A spray of fresh, clean water will help to keep this decoration looking fresh.*

Narcissus Tumblers

Delicate and fragrant, 'Paper White' narcissus are among the first of the prepared winter-flowering bulbs to bloom and their pretty flowers are ideally suited to smaller arrangements.

SMALLER FLOWERS OFTEN require smaller and simpler settings in order to be fully appreciated. 'Paper White' narcissus, for example, have a daintiness and delicacy that can be easily overshadowed, and they will look lost in cavernous surroundings. The fact that these flowers are cosseted and cared for in order to force the early blooms can make them rather expensive, but this project requires only a single bunch to make two decorations. Small pieces of cellophane are crumpled into the glass tumblers, resembling ice, and, as an acknowledgment that Christmas is on the way, a few silver sequin stars are dropped into the water to add a little sparkle. Although narcissus can be dwarfed when used in the same arrangement as larger, showier flowers, here a single amaryllis in its own tumbler serves to accentuate the size and fragility of its neighbor.

Materials used

Highball tumblers

2 pieces of clean cellophane

silver sequin stars (optional)

10 stems of 'Paper White' narcissus

'Paper White' narcissus
(N. papyraceus)

Making the Narcissus Tumblers

I have used two highball style tumblers to create this simple decoration, but any glasses or even glass jars would be suitable. The cellophane should be screwed up tightly into small balls, which may require some coaxing to fit within the containers. Once water is added, tiny pockets of trapped air are formed, giving the cellophane the appearance of crushed ice. These air pockets may cause the cellophane to rise out of the tumblers again; use a pair of scissors to snip through it in places, as this will release some of the air so the cellophane sits within the glass. The narcissus stems are threaded amongst the cellophane and sequins are added as an extra festive and frosty touch.

1 Screw up the pieces of cellophane into fairly small balls and add them to each tumbler. Pour in fresh water so that the glasses are about two-thirds full.

2 Use a wooden skewer to press the cellophane down into the water, if necessary. Add glitter stars to the water, again using the skewer to position them.

3 Cut each stem fairly short and insert the flowers in among the cellophane. Build up the decoration, placing shorter stems around the sides and taller ones in the middle.

Pine Hangings

Rather Shaker-like in their naive simplicity, these three-dimensional hanging decorations are made from sprigs of pine, and look great when hung in a group at a window.

As A CHILD, I used to love bending pieces of wire into interesting shapes and covering them with sparkly tinsel–the brighter and gaudier the better. Those early efforts were the precursors of these somewhat more restrained and tasteful versions, with the glitter of the tinsel replaced by the fragrant and subtle sophistication of pine. These decorations can be made in any number of shapes and sizes. In fact once you have covered a number of lengths of wire, why not give one to each member of the family and allow them to create whatever form they wish. Certainly the results will be original!

Pine *(Pinus sp)*

Materials used

18-gauge florist's stub wires, as long as possible

Short snippings of pine

Florist's reel wire

Ribbon

Baubles

Tips and techniques

Joining stub wires
The easiest and most secure way in which to join two stub wires is to twist them both together at the ends. Allow at least 2 inches (5 cm) at the end of each of the two wires, and twist both at the same time, as shown.

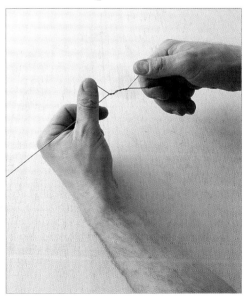

Making the Pine Hangings

You will find it much easier and more time-effective to prepare a pile of pine pieces before you actually begin to attach them to the wires. This way, you can continue with the binding without having to break off every few minutes to cut more stems. This would be an ideal way to use up any branches which have been trimmed from the base of the Christmas tree.

1 Attach the reel wire to the end of one of the stub wires, winding it around several times and pulling tightly as you do so to ensure that it is secure.

2 Bind a sprig of pine to the stub wire with reel wire, winding it between the needles so that it does not show. Place the next sprig over the end of the first and bind again.

3 Keep adding sprigs of pine. Bear in mind that you are aiming for a narrow, slender finished shape and that the strip of covered wire should look nice and even.

4 Having covered several lengths of wire, you can join them to form shapes. Wire a bauble to hang centrally from the top of the decoration and then hang the decorations from ribbons.

Fragrant Freesia Garland and Bowl

The combined scents of pine, cloves, freesias, and oranges makes for a wonderfully evocative and aromatic table setting, which may be easily adapted to suit any table.

WHETHER ADORNING the table for the celebratory Christmas meal, or simply for dinner on a winter's evening, this decorative centerpiece is a feast for the eyes as well as a treat for the nose! Freshly made pomanders of clove-studded tangerines are scattered upon the table around a winding garland of fresh blue pine, shiny dark green holly, and golden yellow freesias. Gilded walnuts add an opulent and luxurious touch. Placed within the center of this elegant garland, a simple yet stunningly perfumed display of open freesias gives weight and substance to the overall effect. These bright flowers are arranged within a container that has been covered with pine tips, echoing the garland. Placed upon a dark oak table, the whole effect is one of simple but well thought-out elegance.

Artless beauty
Traditional Christmas roses (Helleborus niger) are massed within a moss-lined glass bowl, their understated beauty compensating for what appears to be a deliberate lack of arrangement.

Making the Fragrant Freesia Garland and Bowl

Garlands can be made using one of two techniques: by binding the flowers and foliages onto a rope, ribbon, or similar support; or by wiring small, individually wired bunches of plant material to a base formed from moss and chickenwire. The latter method is better suited to larger garlands, which contain bulky and heavy foliage and flowers. This table garland, being rather more delicate and less weighty, is therefore made using the binding method.

I find that preparing all the materials before I begin to assemble the garland helps speed up the whole process enormously. This may seem a little tedious, and there is the temptation to start putting the garland together before all the foliage and flowers are cut. However, it really is much easier to do your groundwork first, rather than have to stop in mid-flow and go in search of extra materials.

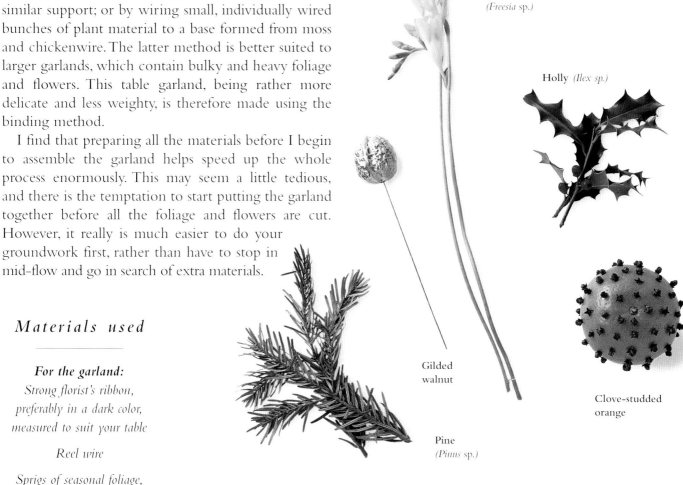

Freesia
(*Freesia* sp.)

Holly (*Ilex* sp.)

Gilded
walnut

Clove-studded
orange

Pine
(*Pinus* sp.)

Materials used

For the garland:

Strong florist's ribbon, preferably in a dark color, measured to suit your table

Reel wire

Sprigs of seasonal foliage, such as pine, holly, etc.

15 stems of double yellow freesias

25 walnuts, gilded

For the freesia-filled bowl:
Soaked flower foam

Straight-sided plastic bowl

Reel wire

12 sprigs of pine

30 stems of double yellow freesias

Adding the walnuts

The shape, color and texture of walnuts make them ideal for adding interest to many arrangements. Here, they are given a coat of gold spray paint. I always advise buying gold and silver spray paints in summer, storing them until December, when shops sell out of supplies within a couple of days.

Spraying the nuts
Push a stub wire into the fleshy join of the shell, insert into florist's foam, and spray.

Attaching the nuts
Using a glue gun, put glue on one end of the nut and press it onto the garland.

1 Attach the reel wire to one end of the ribbon, pulling it tight. Hold a piece of pine flat against the ribbon, bring the wire over it and bind, securing the stem of pine to the ribbon.

2 Add more foliage, keeping each piece flat against the ribbon, covering the stem and binding wire of the previous piece as you go. Add in a stem or two of freesias in the same way.

3 Work all the way along the ribbon, alternating clusters of freesias with sprigs of foliage. Do not bind the freesias too tightly with the wire, or you will cut through their tender stems.

5 Make a small hole near the rim of the bowl with a bradawl or scissors, insert the end of the reel wire through the hole, and twist the wire onto itself a couple of times. Hold a sprig of pine against the side of the bowl and wrap the binding wire around it, adding further sprigs to cover the bowl. Trim the stems so that the base of the bowl is level. Insert soaked flower foam and arrange the freesias into the foam.

4 At the end of the garland, add some foliage stems in the same way but point them in the opposite direction. This gives a neat finish, obscuring any unsightly stems or wires. Add natural and gilded nuts into the garland (see box left).

Pot Plants

FROM SMALL, perfectly formed mounds of fresh, fluffy green *Soleirolia soleirolii* (also known by the inspired name of baby's tears) to exotic and very chic phalaenopsis orchids and velvety, bold-colored gloxinias, plants are an ideal way in which to add some color and freshness to any room in the home. As many plants flower continuously for weeks on end, they are also an excellent value, especially as so many of them can be kept and will come back into flower given a little care and attention. Presented within myriad containers, vases, baskets, or even kitchen cookware, they offer an exciting new range of decorating techniques and effects.

Windowsills

*The windowsill is an ideal place for compact decorations,
especially if there is a garden beyond the window, as the flowers
will appear to bring the garden indoors.*

WHEN CHEERING UP a window, I would choose flowering
plants rather than cut flowers because they last so much
longer and are more versatile. Individual pots of plants, arranged
together, tend to look more attractive than a single, elongated
display, especially on a wide windowsill. You can mix and
match containers in a variety of textures and styles to show off
flowers or plants to their best advantage.

Casual marguerites
French cassoulet bowls (left) are planted with simple marguerite daisies and the compost covered with carpet moss. Placed in a rather formal setting, they add freshness and style, yet still have a casual air.

Pastel-toned auriculas
The delicate auriculas (above) are at the perfect height for closer inspection. Galvanized flowerpot molds make ideal containers as the color of the metal is sympathetic to the mealy dust which occurs on the foliage and flowers.

Spring daffodils
Indoor-reared daffodils (right) are displayed in terra cotta pots painted in pretty pastel shades. The flowers will give weeks of pleasure in early spring if dead-headed regularly. After flowering they may be planted out in the garden.

Steps

With pots of colorful annuals, bright spring bulbs, or flowering winter greenery, careful planting and placement can ensure that outdoor steps will look decorative throughout the year.

WHEN PLANTING containers for steps, almost anything goes, as they provide natural staging. It is sensible to avoid very wide containers or plants if the steps need to be accessed; I would also try to avoid over-use of symmetry, unless you are fortunate enough to have an exceedingly wide staircase. Do be careful with thorny plants, or those with staining, pollen-bearing flowers, as these may pose a hazard as you pass by.

Winter viburnum
A collection of blue ceramic glazed pots have been planted with standard, trained flowering Viburnum tinus *and underplanted with trailing ivy, which has been clipped to form a low mound. These little 'trees' provide winter colour and have pleasingly sculptural shapes.*

Spring bulbs

Baskets woven from natural willow have been heavily varnished to protect them from the spring weather. Lined with sphagnum moss and filled with compost, the two larger baskets have been planted with fragrant pink hyacinths and miniature narcissus. The smallest basket contains winter-flowering Johnny-jump-up, which is very robust. The entire collection will give weeks of enjoyment.

Summer roses

Miniature roses are planted in rustic wooden containers and interspersed with scented-leaved geranium plants in terra cotta pots for a sunny, summery display.

143

Doorways

*Be it the main entrance to your home, a back door
leading onto the garden, or French doors, there is always an
opening for the imaginative use of potted plants.*

FROM A FORMAL townhouse to a humble country cottage,
the doorway is the focal point of a home. Visitors are
always struck by first impressions and are bound to remember
the way plants have been used to create a welcome and to add
a decorative accent. By using clipped boxwoods, a more formal
note is struck, while overflowing pots of colorful summer
flowers lend a more informal and relaxed air.

Winter topiary
*Elegant square terra cotta
pots are planted with clipped
boxwood topiaries and used
to flank each side of this
formal townhouse doorway.
Pots of trailing ivy soften the
effect and, during the summer, may be augmented with
some colorful geraniums or
miniature roses.*

Spring rhododendron
A standard trained rhododendron tree has been planted in a lime-washed pot and finished with a flourish of fresh-looking forget-me-nots. Its gentle coloring and relaxed form is ideal for a simple, rustic doorway and it provides height without being too dominant.

Summer fuchsias
Delicate standard fuchsia plants are always great values during the summer, as they will last for ages if deadheaded regularly. Here, a fuchsia has been planted in a galvanized container, inspired by the steel doorstep tread, and underplanted with miniature trailing fuchsias. Pebbles have been scattered around the base of the container to reflect the cobblestone path edging.

Balconies

Clematis, rambling roses, and annual climbers, such as morning glory and cup-and-saucer vine (Cobaea), all make wonderful decorative coverings for balcony trellises or balustrades.

NO MATTER what their size, balconies provide an ideal chance to bring some of the garden a little nearer to the home. Tall and climbing plants are ideal subjects for screening walls, unsightly views and providing privacy, with smaller annuals and perennials adding moments of color and form. Lightweight containers, such as those made from reconstituted stone or plastic terra cotta, are more suitable for balconies than heavy stone or ceramic pots. Whichever containers you do choose, they should have maximum capacity for soil so that they do not dry out during hot or windy weather. Even the largest of pots, once planted, will need to be throughly watered at least once, if not twice a day, during the hot summer months.

Trained clematis
The delicate and fragrant summer-flowering clematis (left) has been trained over a simple wrought iron railing. Left to its own devices it will form a cover very quickly.

Summer color
A balustrade-enclosed balcony (right) has a summer planting of palest blue cape plumbago (Plumbago auriculata) climbers underplanted with tobacco plants (Nicotiana sp.). In colder climes, the plumbago plants would need to be moved indoors to protect them from winter frosts.

Patios

Pots can be used to great effect on a patio as, unlike permanent planted flower beds or borders, they can be moved and rearranged throughout the year at will.

WHEN POSITIONING pots on the patio, avoid placing them in straight lines around the edges, as this will reinforce the boundaries and make the patio seem smaller and more enclosed. Instead, use pots in groups at the corners and in clusters toward the center of the patio to give interest and break up expanses of hard surface. Remember that even when it rains, pots and containers of plants may still require watering.

Shady characters
*In a corner of a town patio (left), white busy Lizzies (*Impatiens *sp.) and baby's tears (*Soleirolia soleirolii*) are planted in whitewashed pots. Both are shade lovers, so are ideally suited to patios and terraces that get little direct sunlight.*

Terra cotta stack
*A trio of terra cotta pots in descending sizes are assembled one within the other, separated by plenty of compost. Petunia and verbena plants are inserted within the gaps and a flamboyant New Zealand flax (*Phormium *sp.) provides the "finale" in the center of the top pot.*

Small Indoor Plants

A far cry from those dusty rubber plants which crept ever skyward, house plants today provide more subtle opportunities to bring vibrant greenery and color into the home.

AS THE RANGE of plants available for the home grows ever wider, the floral decorator has increasing scope for experimentation. Both flowering and foliage plants can be used as ornaments and accessories that enhance the design or decor of a room, as well as in "tablescapes" that provide color throughout the year.

Indoor plants will last indefinitely if properly cared for. Most plants need to be watered regularly during the flowering period and, once the flowers fade, the plants can be moved to a less conspicuous but still light place.

Sculptural cacti
The extraordinary and strongly shaped cacti (left) provide an ideal foil for the natural, earthy tones of the room. Such an interesting collection can be extended and amassed over the years and has the bonus of requiring next-to-no maintenance.

Streptocarpus basket
Rich-colored cape primroses, or Streptocarpus, (right) are simply placed, in their pots, into a moss-filled basket and fresh green carpet moss added to hide the plastic pots. With a little care and occasional feed, they will flower happily for many weeks.

Large Indoor Plants

A sizeable plant is an eye-catching feature in any room, but it should not be left to run riot. To look their best, some of the larger flowering plants may need to be supported on a frame.

When choosing houseplants, you can often find those that come already fitted with a support, such as the highly scented, flowering jasmine (left), which has been trained over a wire hoop frame and looks both neat and pretty. Many orchids also make ideal houseplants, as they are long-lasting and far less expensive than they used to be. Cymbidium orchids and delicate, elegant phalaenopsis are among my favorites and I often find that they look far more impressive, and last longer, when supported within a glass vase on a very simple willow twig frame.

1 *Remove the orchid plant from its pot. It is usually grown in coarse compost to prevent its roots from becoming waterlogged. Once out of its pot, the loose compost will fall away. Retain a small amount of compost around the root ball.*

2 *Fill a tall glass vase with broken shards of terra cotta and carefully place the root ball of the plant on top. Add more pot shards to secure the root ball and ensure that the plant is in an upright position.*

3 *Place two willow twigs opposite one another in the vase, and push them to the bottom. Use a third twig to support the flower stems, tying it to the two upright twigs and attaching the flower stems to the support with raffia.*

Tall and graceful
The twiggy frame supports the delicate orchid flowers perfectly and the plant will last for weeks on end if the roots are kept moist. Do not overwater, or the roots will rot.

Artificial Flowers

THE BEAUTY of artificial flowers is that they are available all year round, in myriad colors. Nowadays, it is possible to be more inventive with dried or silk decorations than ever before, as new materials and improved technology have given us a far more realistic and extensive range of flowers and foliage to choose from. Indeed, I sometimes find it difficult to tell silk flowers from their fresh counterparts—and, along with dried flowers, when used creatively they are an invaluable aid, offering a longevity and maneuverability that you just cannot get with the real thing.

Introduction

THE FACT THAT the dried flower market has really got its act together means that beautiful, excellently preserved materials are now imported from around the world and are sold in immaculate condition. As a result, those for whom silk and artifical flowers still bring back ghastly memories of dead, sticky brown leaves, dust-covered pampas grass, and violently colored nylon roses may rest assured. These old-style materials have now been relegated to the past.

The silk and artificial flower, foliage and plant manufacturers are now able to offer us an incredible array of stylish, sympathetically produced and accurately copied flowers, many of which defy detection. Artificial flowers must always be chosen with care and with an eye to where they are to be used, as

Poppy-head cone
This stylish conical decoration would look stunning on a mantelpiece. Dried poppy seedheads have been inserted into a cone of dried flower foam, the smaller stems being wired into position to fill any gaps and ensure the mechanics are covered. A circle of felt has been glued to the base of the cone to give a neat finish.

Rustic attraction
Ideal for a kitchen wall or as a house-warming gift, this simple bunch of dried lavender and wheat has been attached to a rustic wooden spoon and fork with reel wire. The wire has been camouflaged with a length of natural cotton cord.

the immediate give-away that you are not using real flowers is to select roses or lilies in shades of bright blue and green that would never appear in nature. As a general rule, try to pick flowers in their natural colors.

The bonus with artificial flowers is that you are able to create any look you desire at any time of the year and, although the initial outlay may be costly, with care and attention these flowers will last for many years.

Dried flowers and foliage are also of superior quality these days. This is partly due to the speed with which they are dried, which means the colors and shapes are barely diminished from when they were in their fresh form. They are also far less expensive than they used to be, as the majority of supplies come from Holland, where flowers are dried quickly and relatively cheaply directly from the growers.

Rosy posy
A delicate Victorian posy-style arrangement is created within a small glass sphere filled with preserved rose petals. Two colors of dried rose heads have been used, and these have been gently steamed to open the flower heads slightly, so increasing their size and effect.

Formal

Celosia Tree

A dramatic and sculptural "tree" is created from velvety, deep burgundy celosia and is set within a container bound by preserved, leathery-looking, burgundy magnolia leaves.

AN IDEAL DECORATION for a dining room, or perhaps a paneled drawing room, this bonsai-like tree is slightly less formal than many of my other ideas because its trunk is made from contorted willow, which lends a softer informality to any arrangement. It is the celosia that provides an element of severity with its strong blocks of color. Although I have used heads of celosia here, other dried flowers and foliage, such as clusters of preserved poppy heads or dried rose flowers, would look equally stunning. However, there is quite a large surface area to be covered, so whichever flower or foliage you choose, it must be in plentiful supply. For a different and more sculptural effect, try using just a single stem as the tree trunk, and make the canopy of the tree cube-shaped or even rectangular.

Flower topiary
This miniature topiary flower tree is created in a similar way to the celosia tree, but along simpler lines. A stem of birchwood supports a sphere of dried flowers (see Rose Topiary Ball, pages 70-73 for method). Short stems of daisies, carnations, and pink and cerise roses are added to the sphere until it is fully covered.

Making the Celosia Tree

To form the levels of canopy on this tree, two pads of moss are attached to the willow trunk at different heights. The base for each pad is made from a scrunched-up piece of chickenwire stuffed with dry sphagnum moss. The moss used should be thoroughly dry, as any moisture will cause mold to develop. You must also make sure that the underside of each pad is well filled with moss to conceal any of the shiny chickenwire. Clusters of celosia are then wired securely to the moss pads, forming a velvety covering.

Celosia comes on a fairly long stem and needs to be cut short and broken down into individual florets, which are then individually wired into small clusters. Although I have placed my finished tree in a container covered in preserved burgundy magnolia leaves, it would look equally attractive in a brass cachepot.

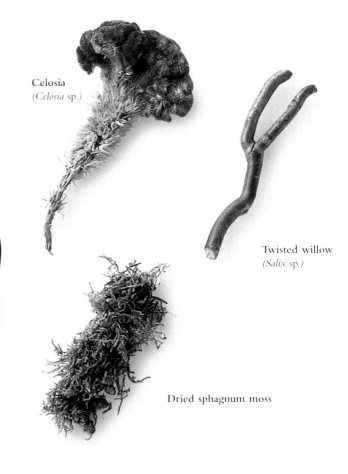

Celosia
(*Celosia* sp.)

Twisted willow
(*Salix* sp.)

Dried sphagnum moss

Preserved
magnolia leaf

Materials used

Plastic container or bucket

Plaster of Paris

Chickenwire

Dried sphagnum moss

Stub wires

Sticky flower fix

Reel wire

3–4 bunches of celosia

3 lengths of twisted willow

10 burgundy preserved
magnolia leaves

Tips and techniques

When using magnolia leaves that have been preserved using glycerine and dye, they can tend to have a sticky, stained coating that should be wiped off.

The celosia should be cut into short stems and divided into florets. The individual florets are then bound together in clusters of three or four using stub wires.

Wiping magnolia leaves
Using a dry paper towel, rub off the sticky coating that covers the magnolia leaves.

Wiring celosia
Separate the celosia into florets and wire 3-4 florets into a cluster.

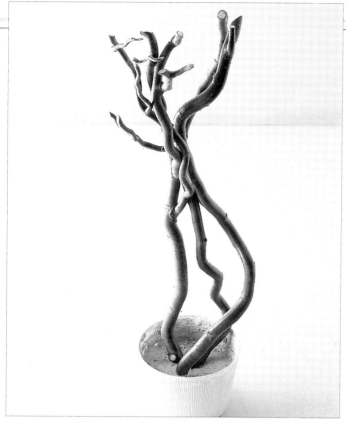

1 *Mix up some plaster of Paris according to the instructions and pour into a straight-sided plastic container. While the cement is wet, arrange the stems into a suitable formation and anchor them securely around the top with a wire until the plaster has set.*

2 *Attach the magnolia leaves to the pot with flower fix, so that each leaf overlaps the next. A reel wire is tied around the leaves for extra security. (Inset) Attach the chickenwire to the tree with reel wire and pack it with moss, paying attention to the underside and ensuring all the wires are concealed.*

3 *Attach the clusters of wired celosia to the moss pad, one at a time. Work around the edge of each pad first to ensure it is covered, allowing the celosia to protrude slightly beneath the pad.*

4 *Fill in each pad, aiming to cover the mechanics with the celosia while creating a flat and compact surface. Any small gaps may be filled in with tiny wired clusters of celosia.*

5 *A second pad of chickenwire and moss is added halfway down the tree. Slightly smaller than the first, it is created in exactly the same way and adds to the finished effect.*

Informal

Garden Flower Pot

It is hard to believe that these flowers are man-made, since they look as if they have just been freshly plucked from the garden. Single stems of flowers add to the informality of the arrangement.

THIS ATTRACTIVE copy of a Victorian terra cotta flower pot contains a delicate and eclectic mix of artificial flowers and foliage, chosen for their interesting shapes, colors and textures and arranged in such a way that their individual beauty may be enjoyed while still working together harmoniously as a whole. Such a style of arrangement can only really be achieved with fresh or silk flowers, since the loose effect requires pliable stems that will form naturally curving arcs. Because dried flowers tend to be much more rigid, it is more difficult to create soft and loose decorations from them. The old rule of using three, five, and seven stems need not apply here for, by including individual flowers, their beauty is amplified, making them more noticeable and striking.

Country air
Equally informal yet arranged in a totally different style, this decoration of dried flowers and foliage in a simple wicker basket has been created within a base of chicken wire. Tall stems of fragrant lavender, roses, and peonies are massed together in true English country-house style.

Making the Garden Flower Pot

Because silk flowers are very light and there is no water involved, this decoration must be created in a heavy container to ensure stability. If you do not have a heavy pot, place some pebbles or dry sand (contained within a small bag) beneath the flower foam. There is no strict ingredients list here, which means you can gradually accumulate an array of artificial flowers as you see those that you like. Building up your collection slowly also makes it easier on the pocket! If you are keen on any one flower, why not make a similar style of arrangement using just the one flower variety. Having filled the pot with dried flower foam, use taller stems of foliage to create the framework, gradually filling in with others and using any that have a trailing habit to gently soften the sides and front.

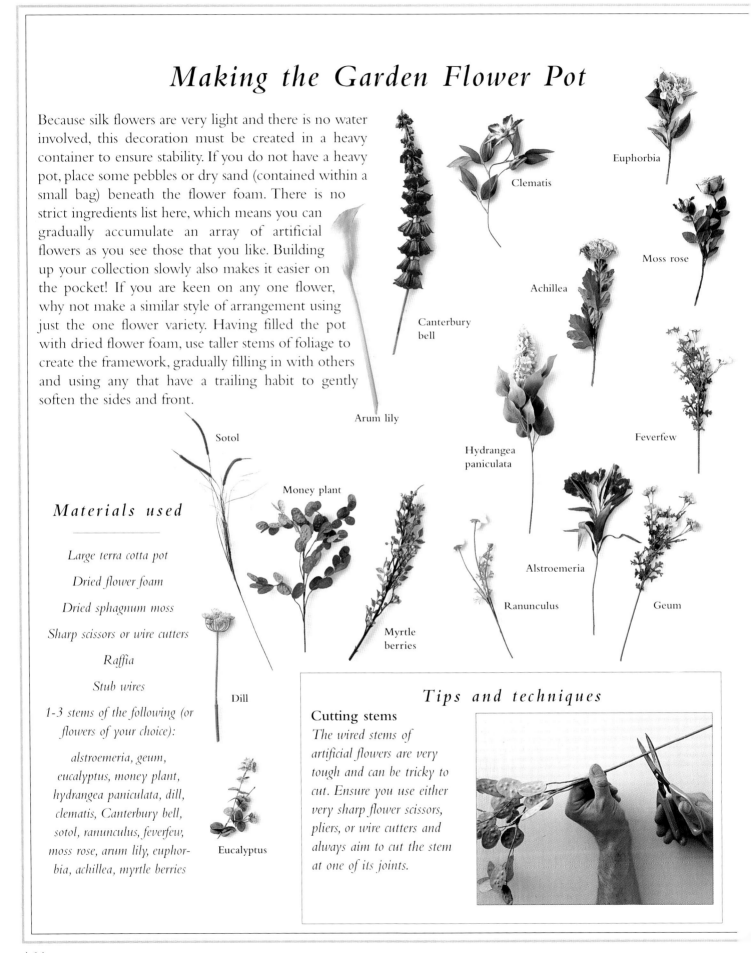

Clematis

Euphorbia

Moss rose

Achillea

Canterbury bell

Arum lily

Sotol

Money plant

Hydrangea paniculata

Feverfew

Alstroemeria

Ranunculus

Geum

Myrtle berries

Dill

Eucalyptus

Materials used

Large terra cotta pot

Dried flower foam

Dried sphagnum moss

Sharp scissors or wire cutters

Raffia

Stub wires

1-3 stems of the following (or flowers of your choice):

alstroemeria, geum, eucalyptus, money plant, hydrangea paniculata, dill, clematis, Canterbury bell, sotol, ranunculus, feverfew, moss rose, arum lily, euphorbia, achillea, myrtle berries

Tips and techniques

Cutting stems
The wired stems of artificial flowers are very tough and can be tricky to cut. Ensure you use either very sharp flower scissors, pliers, or wire cutters and always aim to cut the stem at one of its joints.

1 *Wedge a block of foam into the pot and trim to within 1 inch (2.5 cm) of the rim. Cover the foam with moss, using hairpins of stub wire to secure it. Shape the framework with eucalyptus.*

2 *The money plant is added next and used to establish the framework of your design. The whip-like and elegant arching sprays of sotol are added to soften the edges.*

3 *Continue building the shape with stems of flowers. Make the most of materials like clematis, which have a trailing habit, by placing them to the front of the decoration to soften the rim.*

4 *Tall stems of Canterbury bell are added to give height at the back of the arrangement and a couple of stems of hydrangea paniculata are placed centrally to provide variety of texture, shape, and color.*

5 *The specimen flowers are inserted last, including the elegant blush-pink moss roses, cream ranunculus, and clematis. A single stem of arum lily is placed slightly off-center, allowing its dramatic shape to make a statement.*

Modern

Gerberas in Colored Sand

Bright, bold and simplistically modern, this sand-filled glass bowl contains a sunburst of artificial gerberas, surrounded by a softening halo of delicately arching sotol.

COLORED SAND and gravel is now widely available from good florists and garden centers and can be used to create all manner of effects in simple, clear glass containers. The added bonus is that once you are bored with one design, you can simply tip out the sand and think up another. As with other artifical decorations, it is essential that the container is heavy enough to contain the arrangement without falling over, and here the sand provides an ideal weighty base. If you are unable to find different colored sands, try using pebbles or shells collected from the beach to form an equally interesting effect. In this instance, I have chosen gerberas in colors that do not occur naturally, yet the overall design works because it focuses on their bold, striking form.

Natural distinction
Created in the same fashion as the gerbera arrangement, this decoration comprises entirely natural materials. Dried heads of ornamental artichokes are arranged with clusters of dried phalaris grass in a square glass vase filled with sea-washed pebbles and shells.

Making the Gerberas in Colored Sand

For this decoration, a block of flower foam is placed in a shallow glass bowl and secured with sticky flower fix. Then two different colors of sand are poured in individually to create an attractive, swirling pattern.

If you cannot find different colored sands, one color would serve just as well, as would fine gravel and small pebbles, which could be used in a similar fashion to create a distinct motif. The gerbera daisies are added in bold clumps, with most of the stems cut fairly short in order to produce the effect of a fairly striking mass of color, shape, and texture. The joy of using artificial flowers is that each stem contains a wire that may be bent and manipulated into any shape that you desire. Although I have used a mixture of colors, you could achieve a very dramatic look by sticking to just one or two shades of flower.

The addition of the sotol helps to soften the arrangement and adds an extra element in terms of interesting texture and shape.

Gerberas

Materials used

Block of dried flower foam

Colored sand in two shades, or pebbles

Shallow glass bowl

Sticky flower fix

5 stems of artificial sotol

18 stems of artificial gerberas

Tips and techniques

Many artificial flowers are tightly packaged, since the majority are imported and shippers tend to pack as many as possible into the smallest space to keep costs to a minimum. Once you have bought the flowers it is important to unpack them with care so as to maximize their potential. Gently open the petals or even give them a very light steaming to help them fall into place.

Removing wrapping
Carefully remove the protective plastic wrapping from the flower head.

Opening petals
Fan out the flower head, teasing the petals into shape with your fingers.

1 *Attach the flower foam to the base of the glass container with sticky flower fix. Make sure you leave plenty of space around the foam for the sand or pebbles.*

2 *Pour one color of sand into the bowl, forming interesting contours. Add the next color so as not to disturb the first and use a stick to create swirls on the surface.*

3 *Using longer stems of gerbera first, arrange them around the edge of the bowl to form a framework. These stems should all be roughly the same length to achieve a cohesive and even profile. If you are using a mixture of colors, distribute them evenly throughout the arrangement.*

4 *Continue adding the stems of gerberas color by color, cutting some substantially shorter and recessing them within the heart of the decoration, to lead the eye into the arrangement and create a feeling of depth.*

5 *The final touch is to add the soft and very airy stems of sotol in among the gerberas. These slender grasses will help to enlarge the decoration without adding any weight or heaviness.*

Inexpensive

Hydrangea "Brick"

The mellow, autumnal coloring of the dried hydrangeas is the major attraction of this compact decoration, which would sit perfectly on a narrow shelf or sill.

HYDRANGEA FLOWERS are great favorites of mine and there is an incredible range of colors available. The whole spectrum of shades changes through the autumn and, as the frosts arrive, even more dramatic colors are seen, with deep burgundy, rusts, and blues providing striking fodder for dried or fresh decorations. Hydrangeas are also very easy to dry. You can either hang them upside down in a dark, warm, airy place; or put them in a vase of water and let them slowly transpire until all the water has gone, by which time they should have dried naturally. You can also buy commercially grown and dried hydrangea heads but the colors are more limited and they can get squashed if not packaged and transported with care.

Materials used

3 dried hydrangea heads

Felt or card

Wet flower foam

Dried carpet moss

Stub wires

Scissors

Dried hydrangea
(Hydrangea sp.)

Dried carpet moss

Making the Hydrangea "Brick"

I have used an unsoaked piece of wet flower foam, as it is softer and so makes it easier to insert the stems of the rather brittle dried hydrangeas. You may also use dry foam, but it may be necessary to wire the hydrangea stems to make them easier to insert. For a more formal effect you could substitute dried roses for the hydrangeas, placing them in an upright position, as if they are growing.

1 *Cut a piece of unsoaked wet flower foam to the desired length, (about two-thirds of the block). Glue a piece of felt or card to the base of the block and trim it to size.*

2 *Cover the four sides of the block using dried green carpet moss. Fix it in place at intervals using small "hairpins" of wire.*

3 *Using a pair of sharp scissors, trim around the edges of the carpet moss, both at the top and the base, to ensure that the edges look crisp and neat.*

4 *Push the stems of the hydrangeas into the top of the mossy flower foam brick, until it is covered. Break one head into smaller florets and use these to fill any gaps around the sides.*

Inexpensive

Bamboo Thistles

These sculptural decorations of dried globe thistles and bamboo look exactly like miniature cacti and would make an impressive display in a modern living room, or even in the bathroom.

T HESE DRIED GLOBE thistle heads are an icy blue shade, which perfectly complements the natural parchment-colored bamboo vases. The containers are made from large, dried bamboo, cut into short lengths. If you are unable to obtain the large diameter bamboo, use short lengths of readily available canes and attach them around the sides of a straight-sided container such as a glass tumbler or plastic carton.

The flower heads are very brittle and break easily, so should be treated with care. To dry them, pick the fresh flowers when still in bud, before the trumpet-like petals open. Remove the leaves at the base of each stem and bind the stems together in bunches of no more than ten, secured with a rubber band. If hung upside down in a dark, dry and warm room, they will be ready for use in a few weeks.

Materials used

Large-diameter length of bamboo cane, sawn into short lengths

Dry flower foam

25 stems of globe thistle

Globe thistle
(*Echinops* sp.)

Making the Bamboo Thistles

Hollow bamboo stems make ideal natural vases, especially as the decorations do not need any water, so it does not matter if you are using hollow tubes. Use a sharp saw to cut the trunk, taking great care as the bamboo can splinter and form sharp edges that should be smoothed with a file. The flowers are inserted into the dry flower foam and clumped together so that all the mechanics are hidden.

1 *Cut up some small pieces of dry flower foam and shape the ends to make a slight point for easy insertion into the vases. Wedge the foam very firmly into the bamboo.*

2 *Cut the globe thistles into short lengths and remove any foliage. Arrange the heads to form a compact mound within the bamboo, ensuring that all the flower foam is covered.*

Table setting

Spring Flower Pots

Ideal for a spring luncheon table, assorted silk plants have been arranged as if growing in a collection of pastel-colored pots.

THERE IS ENDLESS scope for creating a huge range of looks with silk flowers and plants. They can be used either on their own or in conjunction with fresh foliage to make decorations that are as beautiful as the real thing but infinitely tougher! Silk flowers may seem expensive, especially when compared to fresh flowers, but they will last for three to four years, continuing to look as good as the day you bought them. If they do get dusty or dirty, they can also be washed—simply give them a swirl in a bowl of warm, soapy water, rinse them off in clean water, and hang them to dry away from direct sunlight and strong winds. Once dry, they will look as good as new.

Naturally pretty
These square terra cotta pots have been filled with bunches of natural dried roses. Placed together in a small group or used individually, they look very effective and would make a lovely gift

Making the Spring Flower Pots

For this decoration, you will need to assemble a variety of small silk flowers and flowering plants that complement one another. I have used both flowers and bulbs and have chosen miniature ceramic pots in soft shades as containers—these are ideal for spring decorations because they look so fresh. I have kept each decoration simple, allowing the interesting shapes of the flowers to predominate. The pots are each filled with small pieces of dried flower foam. This is secured in place using a glue gun. It is important when making dried and artificial flower decorations to ensure that the mechanics are secure, as the arrangements are to last for so much longer. Once the foam is in position, it is covered with dried moss. Each plant is then inserted into its own pot to give the impression that the flowers are growing naturally.

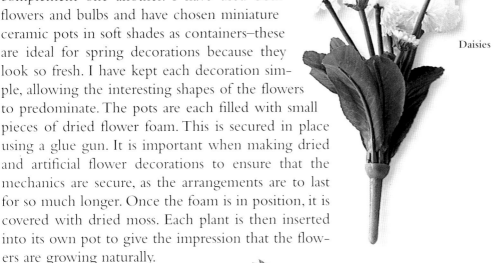

Daisies

Hyacinth

Dandelion

Johnny-jump-up

Materials used

Small pots	1 silk Johnny-jump-up plant
Dry flower foam	1 silk dandelion plant
Dried moss	2 silk daisy plants
Stub wires	2 silk hyacinth bulbs

Tips and techniques

Trimming frayed edges

Because they are made from relatively flimsy materials, some artificial plants and flowers may have a few frayed leaves. Use a pair of very sharp scissors to trim away any tatty edges so that the plants look their best.

1 Cut the flower foam into small cubes that can be wedged inside each pot. Trim the foam to within 1 inch (3 cm) of the rim. Cover the foam with moss, attaching it with hairpins of wire.

2 Unpack the plants and bend the leaves and flowers into a natural shape. Most of the leaves will have a slender wire running through them, allowing you to manipulate them easily.

3 Insert the flowers and plants into the flower foam in each pot, ensuring that they are stable. With the flowering bulbs, allow the bulbous roots to sit above the surface of the moss so that they may be fully enjoyed.

4 With the daisy plants, push them far enough into the foam to cover the plastic base of the leaves. Having arranged the plants in the foam, gently manipulate each of the leaves and flowers so that they look as if they are growing naturally.

5 The miniature Johnny-jump-up is inserted into the foam in single stems, arranged in a cluster to simulate the effect of a growing plant. Once completed, this collection of pots may be used either individually or together to provide a refreshing and attractive table decoration.

Artificial Flower Arranging Basics

Easier to use than their fresh counterparts, artificial flowers can be easily manipulated into shape—and no matter how roughly they are handled, they will always look great.

ARTIFICIAL FLOWERS and foliage can be used in many styles of arrangement, particularly if you have mastered a few techniques to help them look their best. By buying carefully and choosing sensible colors, you can make beautiful decorations that are twice as long-lasting as those made from fresh flowers.

Dyeing Flowers with Tea

Many of the less expensive artificial flowers come in rather harsh, unnatural colors. The way I deal with this is to give the flowers a more subtle patina by dipping them in weak tea and then hanging them up to dry.

1 *Carefully remove the foliage from each flower stem and retain. These will need to be added again once the dipping process is completed.*

2 *Pour hot water into a bowl and add a teabag, allowing it to steep for a few minutes. Remove the teabag and immerse each flower head in the tea so that it absorbs the liquid.*

3 *Lift the flower from the tea and suspend it from a stick, allowing any surplus liquid to drip off. Place the flowers in a warm place to dry before replacing the foliage.*

Tea-stained rose

Wiring Flower Heads

Many artificial flowers have several flower heads to a stem, which makes them a good value but rather difficult to use in certain arrangements. If this is the case, the flower heads are best removed from the main stem and mounted individually.

1 *Using a sharp pair of scissors or wire cutters, remove each of the flowers from the central stem, ensuring that you leave a sufficient length of stem to allow you to attach the mounting wire securely.*

2 *Form a hairpin at one end of the wire, hold it across the stem, and bind the long end of wire around the hairpin.*

Wired
flower heads

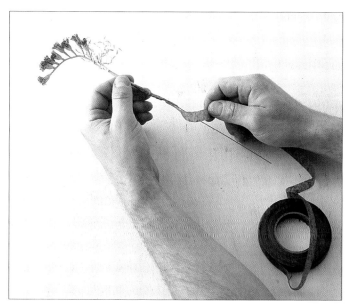

3 *Bind florist's stem tape, which is stretchy and slightly sticky, around each of the wired stems. Twist the stem and pull the tape taught, so that it stretches slightly and forms a tight, green covering that resembles a real stem.*

Neatening Leaves

No matter how expensive, the foliage on artificial flowers can sometimes be less than perfect. Frayed or tatty edges need not present a problem however, as they can be quickly neatened with a pair of sharp scissors.

1 *Carefully examine the leaves on each stem, paying particular attention to strap-like leaves, such as those on hyacinths and alstroemeria, on which any frayed edges will be even more obvious.*

2 *Using very sharp scissors, carefully cut around the edges of any frayed foliage, ensuring you follow the shape of the leaf.*

Neatened leaves on artificial hydrangea paniculata

3 *Work through the leaves so that they all look neat and have cleanly defined edges – this is a fiddly task but one that is very worthwhile if the end result is to look professional and polished.*

Spreading Leaves and Flowers

Most artificial flowers will have been very tightly wrapped. For this reason, it is essential that once purchased, each stem is carefully bent and opened into a more realistic shape. This will also make them look larger in an arrangement.

1 *Carefully slide off the cellophane wrapping, or use scissors to cut through the wrapping if flowers are particularly delicate. Be careful not to mistakenly remove any loose leaves, seeds, flowers, etc.*

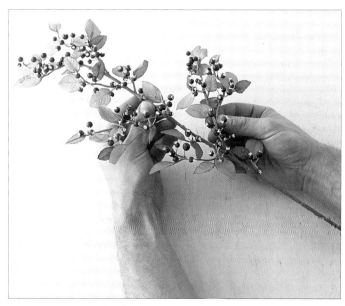

2 *Open out each of the branches, spreading them to their maximum potential and kinking them occasionally to give a more naturalistic effect. Press open the leaves in order to reveal their full shape.*

Open, natural-looking stems

Pressing Flowers

Pressing flowers and leaves is easily done and requires no equipment other than a heavy book or telephone directory. Once flattened, you can use a wide variety of materials to make excellent coverings for containers and vases.

1 *Line the pages to be used inside the book with sheets of white artist's paper. This will prevent petals from being discolored by the print. Place the flowers and leaves upon the page, ensuring that they do not touch one other.*

2 *Carefully close the book, trapping flowers between the pages. Place it to one side beneath a heavy weight, such as several large bricks or other heavy books, and leave for at least four days.*

Pressed lady's mantle leaf

Pressed scabious flowers

Drying Flowers

Drying your own flowers is fun and a good way to use up surplus home-grown material. Almost all flowers are suitable for air-drying provided they are prepared in the correct way and stored in the right conditions.

1 *For best results, dry flowers that are just opening from bud. Remove all the lower leaves from each stem, together with any damaged flowers. By doing this you will prevent any mold occurring once the bunch is hung up to dry.*

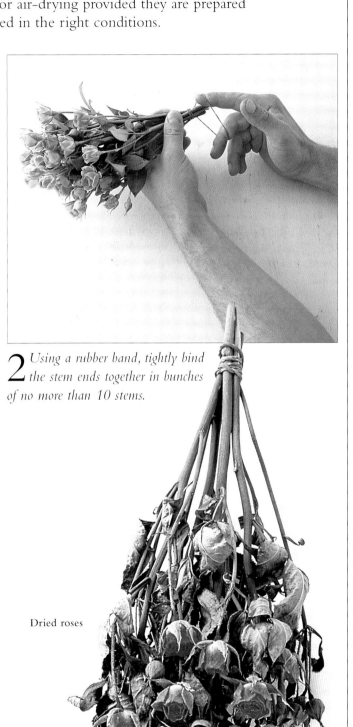

2 *Using a rubber band, tightly bind the stem ends together in bunches of no more than 10 stems.*

Dried roses

3 *Insert a length of stub wire underneath the rubber band and through the stems and bend the end to form a hook. Hang the flowers in a dark, airy room or airing cupboard and leave for several days, or until crisp.*

Flower Lists

Listed on these pages are some of the best flowers, foliage, and potted plants with which to decorate the home. Fresh flowers that are also available dried, or are suitable for drying, are starred (★) for easy reference.

Flowers by season

Spring

Daffodil (*Narcissus* sp.)
Tulip (*Tulipa* sp.)
Buttercup (*Ranunculus* sp.)
Grape hyacinth (*Muscari* sp.)
Crown imperial (*Fritillaria imperialis*)
Iris (*Iris* sp.)
Anemone (*Anemone* sp.)
Freesia (*Freesia* sp.)
Primrose (*Polyanthus* sp.)
Pansy (*Viola* sp.)
Cyclamen (*Cyclamen* sp.)
Euphorbia (*Euphorbia* sp.) – foliage
Whitebeam (*Sorbus aria*) – foliage
Viburnum (*Viburnum opulus*) – foliage

Summer

Rose (*Rosa* sp.)
Peony (*Paeonia* sp.)
Lily (*Lilium* sp.)
Delphinium (*Delphinium* sp.)
Cornflower (*Centaurea* sp.)
Carnation (*Dianthus* sp.)
Marigold (*Calendula* sp.)
Sweet pea (*Lathyrus odoratus*)
Snapdragon (*Antirrhinum* sp.)
Foxglove (*Digitalis* sp.)
Poppy (*Papaver orientalis*)
Philadelphus sp.
Columbine (*Aquilegia* sp.)
Stock (*Matthiola* sp.)
Larkspur (*Consolida* sp.)
Dahlia (*Dahlia* sp.)

Ornamental allium (*Allium* sp.)
Alstroemeria (*Alstroemeria* sp.)
Pink (*Dianthus* sp.)
Lavender (*Lavandula* sp.)
Sweet William (*Dianthus barbatus*)
Love-in-a-mist (*Nigella damascena*)
Zinnia (*Zinnia* sp.)
Lady's-mantle (*Alchemilla mollis*)
Solomon's seal (*Polygonatum* sp.) – foliage
Love-lies-bleeding (*Amaranthus caudatus*) – foliage
Hosta (*Hosta* sp.) – foliage

Autumn

Achillea (*Achillea* sp.)
Chrysanthemum sp.
Money plant (*Lunaria* sp.) – seed heads
Pyracantha (*Pyracantha* sp.) – berries and leaves
Nerine (*Nerinus bowdenii*)
Gladioli (*Gladiolus* sp.)
New York aster (*Aster* sp.)
Hydrangea (*Hydrangea* sp.)
Hypericum sp. – leaves
Cotoneaster sp. – leaves
Birch twigs (*Betula* sp.)

Winter

Amaryllis (*Hippeastrum* sp.)
Hellebore (*Helleborus* sp.)
Snowdrops (*Galanthus nivalis*)

Miniature daffodils (*Narcissus* sp.)
Freesias (*Freesia* sp.)
Holly (*Ilex* sp.) – leaves and berries
Viburnum sp. – leaves and berries
Senecio greyii – foliage
Ivy (*Hedera* sp.) – foliage
Fatsia japonica – foliage and berries
Mahonia sp. – foliage and berries
Dogwood (*Cornus* sp.) – stems

Flowers by color

White

Freesia (*Freesia* sp.)
Tulip (*Tulipa* sp.)
Snowdrop (*Galanthus nivalis*)
Chrysanthemum sp.★
Rose (*Rosa rugosa* 'Alba')★
Hellebore (*Helleborus* sp.)
Daisy (*Bellis perennis*)
Achillea ptarmica 'The Pearl' ★
Geranium phaeum 'Alba'
Lisianthus (*Eustoma grandiflora*)
Laurustinus (*Viburnum tinus*)
Campion (*Silene fimbriata*)
Bridal wreath (*Spiraea* 'Arguta')

Yellows and oranges

Yarrow (*Achillea filipendulina* 'Coronation Gold')★
Daffodil (*Narcissus* sp.)

Sunflower
(*Helianthus* sp.)★
Rose (*Rosa*
'Maigold')★
Golden arum lily
(*Zantedeschia
elliottiana*)
Kangaroo paw
(*Anigozanthos
flavidus*)
Day lily (*Hemerocallis*
sp.)
Glory lily (*Gloriosa superba*)
Peruvian lily (*Alstroemeria* sp).
Polyanthus (*Primula* sp.)
Forsythia (*Forsythia* sp.)
Persian buttercup (*Ranunculus
asiaticus*)★
Double meadow buttercup
(*Ranunculus acris* 'Flore Pleno')★
Cushion spurge (*Euphorbia
polychroma*)
Gerbera (*Gerbera* sp.)
Marigold (*Calendula officinalis*)
Golden rod (*Solidago* sp.)
Mimosa (*Acacia longifolia*)★

Reds and pinks
Flamingo flowers (*Anthurium
scherzeranium*)
Columbine (*Aquilegia* sp.)
Curcuma sp.
Peony (*Paeonia* 'Defender')★
Lobelia 'Cherry Ripe'
Poppy (*Papaver orientale*)
Red and green kangaroo paw
(*Anigozanthos manglesii*)
New York aster (*Aster
novi-belgii* 'Jenny')
Primula (*Primula* 'Captain's
Blood')
Carnation (*Dianthus* sp.)★
Coral flower (*Heuchera* x
brizoides 'Red Spangles')

Rose (*Rosa* 'Red Moss')
Ornamental allium (*Allium
schoenoprasum*)
Sunflower
(*Helianthus* sp.)★
Sweet pea
(*Lathyrus odoratus*)
Love-lies-bleeding
(*Amaranthus caudatus*)★
Gerbera (*Gerbera jamesonii*)
Celosia (*Celosia argentea*
var. *cristata*)★
Statice (*Limonium sinuatum*)★

Blues and purples
Delphinium (*Delphinium* 'Blue
Dawn')★
Polyanthus (*Primula* sp.)
Monkshood (*Aconitum
paniculatum*)★
Dutch iris (*Iris* sp.)
Hyacinth (*Hyacinthus
orientalis*)
Grape hyacinth (*Muscari*
sp.)
Pansy (*Viola* x *wittrockiana*)
Lavender (*Lavandula* angustifolia
'Hidcote')
Globe thistle (*Echinops ritro*
'Veitch's Blue')★
Bellflower
(*Campanula* sp.)
Scabious (*Scabiosa
atropurpurea*, Cockade Series)★
Love-in-a-mist (*Nigella damascena*)
Cornflower (*Centurea cyanus*)★
Bluebell (*Hyacinthoides non-scripta*)
Statice (*Limonium sinuatum*)★

Pot plants

Spring
Amaryllis (*Hippeastrum* sp.)
Azalea (*Rhododendron simsii*)

Blue-flowered torch (*Tillandsia
lindenii*)
Lotus berthelotti
Narcissus cvs.
Clivia minata
Flamingo flower (*Anthurium
scherzerianum*)
Tulips (*Tulipa* sp.)
Shrubby verbena (*Lantana camara*)
Hydrangea (*Hydrangea macrophylla*)
Primrose (*Primula obconica*)

Summer–autumn
Begonia (*Begonia bowerae*)
Brazilian jasmine (*Mandevilla sanderi*)
Busy lizzy (*Impatiens* cvs.)
Lily (*Lilium* sp.)
Orchid (*Cymbidium*
hybrids)
Gerbera (*Gerbera
jamesonii*)
Cape leadwort
(*Plumbago auriculata*)
Persian violet
(*Exacum affine*)
Marguerite (*Argyranthemum
frutescens*)
Golden trumpet (*Allamanda cathartica*)
Cape primrose (*Streptocarpus* cvs.)
Fuchsia (*Fuchsia* sp.)
Verbena (*Verbena* sp.)

Winter
African violet (*Saintpaulia* cvs.)
Viburnum tinus
Jasmine (*Jasminum polyanthum*)
Christmas cactus (*Schlumbergera* sp.)
Begonia (*Begonia* x *hiemalis*)
Cyclamen (*Cyclamen persicum*)
Azalea (*Rhododendron simsii*)
Chrysanthemum (*Argyranthemum* sp.)
Poinsettia (*Euphorbia pulcherrima*)
Peace lily (*Spathyphyllum wallisi*)
Monkey plant (*Ruellia makoyana*)

Glossary

Annual
A plant that completes its life cycle, from setting seed to flowering and then dying, within a single growing season.

Air-drying
A method of drying flowers by hanging them up in a cool, airy place so that they gradually lose all their moisture.

Bradawl
A small, boring tool.

Bulb
A plant storage organ, usually formed underground, containing the growth buds for the following year.

Cachepot
An ornamental flower pot that encloses a common, or more ordinary one.

Cone
The clustered flowers or woody, seed-bearing structures of conifers, e.g., pine.

Climber
A plant that uses other plants or objects to grow upward by means of leaf stalks, aerial roots, suckering pads, twining tendrils, or coiling stems.

Condition
To prepare cut flowers by standing them in cool, clean water, stripping them of lower leaves, or any other treatment to help them last longer in a floral display.

Deadhead
To remove dead flower heads in order to promote further flowering, or improve appearance. Flowers that have several heads on a stem will last longer if the faded blossoms are removed.

Evergreen
A plant that retains its leaves at the end of the growing season, although it may lose leaves throughout the year Semi-evergreen plants retain only some leaves, or lose older leaves only when new growth is produced.

Flower foam
Sometimes known as oasis, this is a soft, permeable material that is available in dry or wet form, and used for holding cut flowers in place in a floral arrangement.

Framework
The basic shape or the structure of a floral decoration, usually created first with foliage and/or taller flowers and then filled in with the remaining ingredients.

Herbaceous
Dying down at the end of the growing season.

Mealy dust
A powdery, white dust that can be the effect of the mealy bug, which is a hothouse pest.

Mechanics
The nuts and bolts of a floral decoration, such as chickenwire and flower foam, which should eventually be disguised

Perennial
A plant that lives for longer than two seasons.

Root ball
The roots together with the soil adhering to them when a plant is lifted, e.g., when repotting.

Sphagnum moss
A moss that often grows in bogs–its moisture-retentive qualities make it extremely useful for floral decorations.

Standard
A tree or shrub with a length of bare stem below the first branches. Shrubs such as roses and fuchsias can be trained to form standards.

Topiary
A form of pruning, training, and clipping plants into artificial shapes. Plants most suited to topiary are small-leaved, slow-growing evergreens.

Woody stemmed
Having a stem composed of tough, woody fibers–such stems often have difficulty in drawing up water when cut for use in flower arrangements.

Suppliers

Nurseries and Mail-Order Catalogues

W. Atlee Burpee Company
300 Park Avenue, Warminster, PA 18974

Calyx & Corolla
185 Berry Street, Suite 6200, San Francisco, CA 94107

Heirloom Old Garden Roses
24062 N.E. Riverside, St. Paul, OR 97137

Heritage Rose Gardens
16831 Mitchell Creek Drive, Fort Bragg, CA 95437

Jackson & Perkins
P.O. Box 1028, Medford, OR 97501

Park Seed Company
Cokesbury Road, Greenwood, SC 29647

Shepherd's Garden Seeds
30 Irene Street, Torrington, Connecticut 06790

Wayside Gardens
1 Garden Lane, Hodges, SC 29695-0001

White Flower Farm
Route 63, P.O. Box 50, Litchfield, CT 06759-0050

Organizations

American Horticultural Society
7931 E. Boulevard Drive, Alexandria, VA 22308

American Institute of Floral Designers
720 Light Street, Baltimore, MD 21230

Index

Acknowledgments

I have gained immense pleasure and satisfaction from working on this title and would like to express my most sincere and grateful thanks to the many people involved in its creation.

I am highly indebted to Susan Berry at Collins & Brown, for her support throughout and to the unflappable Mandy Lebentz, who has been a constant and most loyal editor, guide and friend.

My thanks must also go to Amanda Heywood, for turning my arrangements into stunningly composed photographs, and to her assistant Vanessa Kellas, who, among other tasks, helped prepare so many scrummy lunches! Thank you to Michelle Garrett for her beautiful pictures and to Kevin Williams for his careful layouts and design work.

Throughout New Covent Garden market there are so many friends who work upon the various stands, whom I encounter on a daily basis and who are stalwart in their attempts to satisfy my somewhat demanding flower requirements. Special thanks to David, Ian and John at Baker Duguid, Melvin and Charlie at Romede and Brian and Grant at Q-Ten, along with the two Davids, Graham and Dean at A & F Bacon. I also wish to thank Wayne and his team at Something Special and Pat, Angie and the boys at C. Best.

For being the best packer of a van I have ever met, and for his own special brand of humour, thanks to Roy Steptoe.

The "home team" must also be given huge thanks. Jon Poulsom, ably assisted by Ruth Harris keep my day-to-day business running smoothly and efficiently, while still coping with my neverending demands and requests, and helping to keep my feet firmly on the ground. They and I are grateful to the devoted assistance given by Johnny Atkinson, Dean Cobb, Jaynie Heynes, Jill Roch and the stupendous Catherine Hart.

As ever, I keep my final thanks, which I am never truly able to put into words, for Nicholas, "Hugely and Always."

Picture credits:
Michelle Garrett: p.2, pp.26–27, p.20, pp.146–147